# A NEW HAPPINESS

Christ's Pattern for Living in Today's World

# Gavin Reid

Nashville     ABINGDON PRESS     New York

# A NEW HAPPINESS

*Library of Congress Cataloging in Publication Data*

REID, GAVIN.
  A new happiness.
  1. Beatitudes. 2. Christian life—Anglican
authors. I. Title.
BT382.R395 1976      248'.48'3      75-26504
           *ISBN 0-687-27785-X*

MANUFACTURED BY THE PARTHENON PRESS AT
NASHVILLE, TENNESSEE, UNITED STATES OF AMERICA

For Stephen, Stuart, and Catherine
with grateful thanks for all the happiness
they have brought their mother and myself.
Peace, however, is another matter!

# INTRODUCTION

For me to write a book on the Beatitudes is a clear case of fools rushing in where angels fear to tread. I will say that before anyone else does!

Yet I am entirely unrepentant. The Beatitudes are the purest gold of the Bible and greater expositors than I will ever be have mined them with profit for all. I wrote this book not to try to do better but, quite simply, because I felt I had to. I believe it is better to fail in an attempt to do something great than to succeed in an attempt to do something ordinary. Further, I believe that it is impossible to think around the meaning and message of the Beatitudes and not to come up with something worth sharing. Those words of Jesus are so rich and profound that the word of God cannot but shine through.

My purpose is to try to make Jesus speak them again to the contemporary people of my time. I believe our civilization in the West is at a crossroads, because we have tried to believe in Christ *and* in our own cultural and political sense of values. We have made too little attempt to unscramble one from the other. The result is that in public Christians are too uncertain of their distinctive contribution and motivation—and in our personal lives so many of us are looking in the wrong direction for happiness. Like the Beatitudes themselves, the chapters of this book are meant to open up thought rather than to close it. No one will ever fully sum up the full meaning of Christ's words.

I would like to thank Edward England of Hodder & Stoughton for being so patient with me when this book took so much longer to write than I expected. I would also like to especially thank Elizabeth Bullock who came to my rescue late in the day when I needed someone to decipher my scrawl and type the manuscript. Blessed, indeed, are the merciful!

GAVIN REID
March 1, 1974

# CONTENTS

# CHAPTER 1
## *OUT OF THE FOOL'S PARADISE*

Somewhere toward the end of May in 1967—I remember it well—I lost my old happiness.

I do not say this for effect. It happens to be true and to be one of those turning points in one's personal journey through life that remain firmly in the memory.

My personal story is magnificently unexciting and unimportant. An autobiography would be of little value to anyone, but I want to share this particular episode because I feel the world is full of ordinary people like me who may well be facing, or have to face, similar moments of truth.

At that time I was celebrating my thirty-third birthday. I was (and am) an Anglican clergyman of a strongly evangelical flavor and had just completed my first year in a fascinating and enjoyable job which was bringing me into daily contact with a host of interesting people. I was enjoying myself immensely. I was in frequent demand as a speaker at conferences and special services, and it would appear that, by the grace of God, I had some gifts to exercise in these engagements.

I was a married man of some eight years with my third child a year old and my two elder children charging around full of life and fun. I had—and still have—a wonderful and attractive wife. I had recently moved into an area where my wife and I were able to renew acquaintance with our many childhood friends. They were sunny days, and our new house was a delight to live in with its large garden and set in its pleasant neighborhood.

Above all there was my humor. My brother and I were both gifted—if that is the right word—with a strong sense of the ridiculous. I loved to poke fun at things, to engage in repartee, to lace my sermons with humorous anecdotes, to impersonate others, and so on. Well disposed friends would say that I was irrepressible; others—more realistic perhaps—would say that I was somewhat impossible! There are many Christians who find humor a puzzling business, and as a Christian minister I had fallen foul of such brethren from time to time. There had been hurtful moments, but in the main I enjoyed trying to look for the funny side of life.

I was completely sure that I was a happy person. I was not rich, but I was comfortable enough. I was not famous, but there were good friends and many who said kind things about me. I had my health, and I had my faith in a God of love.

Then in May, 1967, a series of moves in the Middle East took place. I had always read newspapers avidly and tried to keep abreast of world events. I have long believed that the basic truths about the ways of God and the ways of men are best illustrated in international happenings. What could better illustrate human sinfulness than a situation like Vietnam or Northern Ireland? So it was that when the United Nations peace-keeping force left Sinai and the Egyptian army moved up I could see very big trouble brewing. It is of no consequence whether my analysis of the situation was right, sensible, or balanced. The fact was that I believed that war between Egypt and Israel was inevitable and that if Egypt and the Arabs opened hostilities with success the United States would become involved, and that in the light of Russian statements being made, the other big world power could not remain detached.

In short I became convinced that nuclear war on a global scale was imminent. As I have said, it is immaterial whether this was in fact the case. The point is that I came to believe it.

For some three weeks I could hardly sleep and could not concentrate upon my work. My mind alternated between trying to see how to resolve the crisis that was headlined in every newspaper and trying to work out a safe place to which I could take my family should the bombs begin to fall. I kept my car filled up with gas.

Images kept filling my mind. Images of my children searching bewilderedly in the rubble of our home looking for their parents. There was no happiness now. I found comfort in the family and my church, but I did not dare to say what was on my mind. Those days were the loneliest I have so far encountered. They were warm and sunny days, but there was only winter in my soul.

Of course we know that the crisis passed at dreadful cost to the Arab armies. Nobody ever wins a war. But as the tension eased I did not regain the sort of happiness I had enjoyed before. Indeed I have not since rediscovered it. What is more, I do not want to, because what I once had is not worth the keeping.

The old happiness was the fool's paradise. The more I think back the more I can see this. It was partly the exultation of youth. But youth is a very temporary matter. A happiness that depends on a man or woman having more earthly days ahead than behind is a poor sort of happiness. We need to see this clearly today in a time when youthfulness is treasured. I remember seeing a television commercial for a hair dye that could cover up grayness. The message was that it could take years off one's age. Nothing could be more pitiful than even marginally to believe such a message. One is constantly seeing advertisements for baldness cures or wigs. The cosmetics of youthlikeness is a boom industry. But as Jesus said years ago—"which one of you can live a few years more by worrying about it?" (Matt. 6:27 TEV).

I often meet groups of young Christians and note the apparent happiness that they seem to generate. My quiet reflection, however, is that a large element of their corporate happiness is the exultation of youth rather than a rejoicing in the Spirit. Perhaps it is very hard for a young person to find what I now believe is the real happiness.

Another element in my old happiness was my

affluence. I had material possessions to play with and enjoy—a car, gadgets, comfortable furniture, television, warmth in the winter months, and so on. I was a total but unwitting hypocrite. I preached that man did not live by bread alone; but what, in fact, I practiced was exactly such a way of life. What was making me happy was what was making everybody else happy. I remember that May, 1967, was when we purchased our first automatic washing machine. Bliss indeed!

I do not reproach myself in any way for this materialism. I had not consciously chosen it. I had simply and subtly succumbed to it. I was not aware of my hypocrisy. There is probably more guilt in my life now on this matter than there was then. Materialism—the worship of mammon—is the subtlest of the false gods. In a consumer society like mine, it is practically the government-approved religion for the "consumer-led boom" is often chosen by politicians as the way to create overall prosperity.

I remember an advertising campaign many years ago which used the slogan "BRING HAPPINESS INTO YOUR HOME WITH NEW FURNITURE— NOW." What a lie! Whenever I remember this slogan my mind also recalls a visit I made to try to comfort a young widow whose husband had dropped dead during the Christmas holiday. I found her surrounded by the most luxurious home I had visited in the parish where I was ministering. But her deep-pile fitted carpets and stylish chairs brought her no comfort as she mourned the loss of a husband who had appeared to be youthful, successful, and of some wealth.

A third element in my old happiness was a sense of being in control of my world. Of course for this to be the case I had effectively narrowed down my personal world to very small proportions. It consisted of my job, my future plans and prospects, my family, my church, and my friends. It was the world within which I spent all of my time and which completely filled my consciousness.

The possibility of war broke down the walls that protected my personal world from what existed outside. Here were factors that I could never control. I might have felt that I could control my personal plans but I could never control armies and politicians in another part of the world. Much of the deep gloom I felt was linked to frustration and rage that I could not control my circumstances.

It is comparatively easy to develop an "all is well with the world" feeling if you have created a tiny world so orientated that you are always in the middle of it. To find a happiness that can survive a situation where one's whole being is at the mercy of elements totally beyond one's control is quite another matter. As I look back over old sermon notes I can see that my preaching in the early sixties was full of reference to the possibilities of world war. I must have preached about those possibilities without really feeling in my bones that they would ever materialize. When the possibility of war (as I saw it) did in fact break into my consciousness I was enraged and

14

frustrated about something I ought to have met without surprise.

But no—my world was a cheerful busy world of Christian activity into which world and major social issues rarely impinged. There were, after all, sermons to prepare, the youth fellowship to run, holiday conferences to plan, family holidays to arrange, meetings to address, prayers to say, reading (theological) to ponder over, a wife to embrace, children to play with, letters on the office desk to answer, overlong pseudo-intellectual conversations on the state of the church to engage in, and much else. All was well with my little world, and I was hardly aware that any other world existed.

My old happiness, therefore, depended on my living out an unreal life in an unreal world. In this I was no different from someone whose world is one of the tennis club or trade union or work and the company, or anything which blinds the participant from seeing himself as someone very small at the mercy of elements beyond his control. Perhaps we live unreal lives because we have glimpsed how awesome real life and the real world happens to be.

Finally I can now see that my old happiness was partly because I had eliminated any serious thinking about death. In this I was aided by a surrounding society which has set out to veto death as a topic of socailly approved conversation and which has fairly effectively swept it out of our awareness. Death is now something happening to other people in the newspapers, on radio and television. It is part of the plots of plays and books. But when it happens near to hand the funeral directors move in neatly and quickly and sweep the awesome happening out of our awareness as soon as possible.

As Simon Starkey has pointed out in his book *When Death Comes Home* (London: Mowbray, 1972), death in the family can lead to the family becoming outcasts among their neighbors. The trouble is not that we are callous and cruel. It is just that we do not know what to say or how to cope with death close at hand. A doctor friend of mine once said, "Most of my patients are kidding themselves that they are immortal!"

That is exactly what I had been doing, and when I was confronted with the possibility of death all my genuinely held religious theory could not comfort me. The theory could not enter the basic consciousness that was built up by a life lived out, day after day, without the awareness that death would ever happen to me and mine. Of course I believed in heaven and the afterlife. The trouble was that it held no appeal for me whatsoever. I was building a happiness based on what this life could give, and I liked it. I found it hard to be convinced that I would find anything better.

As the months passed, from my personal desolation and the destruction of my old happiness I knew I could not pick up the old pieces and put them back together as before. It was in those months that followed the so-called Six-Day War that I began finding myself drawn to read and ponder over the

Beatitudes—that string of remarkable statements with which Jesus opens the Sermon on the Mount.

> Blessed are the poor in spirit, for theirs is the kingdom of heaven.
> Blessed are those who mourn, for they shall be comforted.
> Blessed are the meek, for they shall inherit the earth.
> Blessed are those who hunger and thirst for righteousness, for they shall be satisfied.
> Blessed are the merciful, for they shall obtain mercy.
> Blessed are the pure in heart, for they shall see God.
> Blessed are the peacemakers, for they shall be called sons of God.
> Blessed are those who are persecuted for righteousness' sake, for theirs is the kingdom of heaven.

I cannot pretend that my growing interest in the Beatitudes was part of a conscious search for a new happiness to replace the old. My interest was, if anything, more concerned with the Beatitudes as a program for living. They spoke about the attitudes and goals required in *being* a Christian, and I have long felt that many Christians (especially those of us who are evangelicals) have thought more about *becoming* a Christian than actually *being* one. The Beatitudes seemed to speak of the particular life-style of the follower of Christ. It was only comparatively recently that it dawned on me that the Beatitudes *are about happiness.* Yet the blessedness (the God-given happiness) of which Jesus spoke was a curious brand. It was a very different happiness from the kind that had once buoyed me up for years but was now gone forever.

## A NEW HAPPINESS

No one considering the participation of a man aware of his own inner poverty in a world ready to persecute him for a righteousness he is determined to pursue, can say that we are talking about a fool in his fool's paradise. Fool he may be in many eyes—but there is no paradise here. Yet this is part of the picture of the blessed man that Jesus describes. I began to see that the words spoke of a realistic world within which a new happiness could be discovered—a happiness without fantasy.

And as I have thought further I have not only seen that Jesus talks about a happiness set against a realistic backdrop. I have seen that he speaks about very relevant and contemporary issues. I do not think these paradoxical statements are meant to be analyzed closely. I think Jesus used the words, as he did in the parables, to start off trains of thought in our minds. As I have considered the Beatitudes over the past few years I have seen that out of the intensely Christ-like atmosphere they generate, certain key issues of life emerge. There is the issue of coming to terms with one's self. There is the matter of coming to terms with one's neighbor. There is the problem of facing the reality of a corrupted and disorientated society. There is the issue of the use and abuse of power. All these themes are built into the Beatitudes, and in this book we shall not attempt to analyze Christ's words line by line but rather to isolate these built-in issues and discern the drift of the Lord's teaching in respect to them.

In doing this I hope we will learn something about

what it means to *be* a Chrisian in the contemporary world, and I further believe we shall learn the secret of a new happiness.

But first there are a few lessons to be learned from the very setting of the Beatitudes that have much to teach those of us who are concerned about the relationship of Christians to those who surround them. Those who so wish may ignore the next chapter and move on to chapter three. But in so doing I think they will miss something. The new happiness of which Jesus spoke is not a private experience. It is part and parcel of a new way of life which is lived out in the fellowship of a new family. This immediately poses questions as to how we Christians understand ourselves and how we are meant to understand those who are not of our number. Some may feel that this has nothing to do with happiness which is the subject of this book. The answer here is that Jesus taught that you cannot isolate happiness. It is something that emerges from living realistic lives, and this living will be in companionship with those of like mind and faith and also in contrast to those who are not. The next chapter may be more "churchy" but the teaching of Jesus on happiness gives us no choice!

# CHAPTER 2
## THE CHRISTIANS, THE CROWDS, AND THE CURIOUS

To whom were the Beatitudes addressed? The answer is—the disciples; the Master's first followers.

> Seeing the crowds, he went up on the mountain, and when he sat down his disciples came to him. And he opened his mouth and taught them . . .

Many commentators see in Jesus' actions a deliberately contrived parallel to Moses going up the slopes of Sinai to receive the Law of God. Here, we are told, is the same God in Jesus giving the new law for his new people—the disciples of Christ. This may well be the case. Certainly the setting seems to be deliberate. The disciples of Jesus are singled out from the hordes of sightseers and gathered around their Master, who takes his seat in the manner of the religious teachers of the day. The words that were to follow were not for the curious (though I believe they were probably overheard by many and this was equally deliberate). Jesus was saying by the very setting of his teaching, "These words are for those who want to be associated with me and all that I stand for; therefore these words are about whatever I am about."

This is important to grasp. The Beatitudes are *not* the entry requirements into the ranks of Jesus' followers. They are much more the set of objectives and attitudes for those who are already his followers. The entry requirements themselves were no more (but no less) than the honest decision of those men who had met Jesus, to join up with his cause and see where it led them. Those entrance requirements are still the same—an honest decision to follow the same Jesus, in as much as we can see him with the inner eye of faith, and work out where he is leading us.

So then when Jesus has a follower, he holds up a set of profound objectives as to how such a person should live. To us a contemporary and helpful phrase, Jesus teaches a *life-style*.

I'm convinced that this is something where Christianity through the centuries has often fallen short. We have frequently suggested to the newly committed that the next step was some pattern of attendance at worship or system of practicing piety. Others of us have wanted to make sure that the new convert had a sound ground in doctrines— conceived, as often as not, in bookish terms. But what these Beatitudes are about is *living*, not theoretical thinking, studying, or adopting particular patterns of praying.

We may well be touching, at this point, on what is a stumbling-block to the significant number of people who are critical of the general values and life-style of contemporary Western society. They are looking for an alternative society or a counter-culture, and what they have come to believe about Christianity is that it offers no more than ideas to tuck away in the mind and devotional practices to fill up Sundays. They do not see a gospel in the message of a crucified Jesus. That seems to be past history and irrelevance. But they might well find something compelling in Jesus as the giver of a new law that challenged the world's assumptions of respectable living with a more total and human life-style. This, to me, is what the Beatitudes are all about. This, to me, is why they matter now. I do not say this to undermine the cross, but to show that Jesus is good news in more ways than one.

Christianity is being misjudged as irrelevant because it is being seen as something unrelated to the problems of personal identity, relationships with others, ambition and power, justice and peace, and so on. Certainly a Christianity epitomized by books and abstract doctrine is irrelevant, as is a Christianity epitomized by private prayers or public ceremonies. But the Christianity Jesus established was about living totally, dangerously, and even painfully in a real world—and this is more relevant than any of today's counter-culture dreams.

So then Jesus had teaching to offer his first followers concerning *the way they should live*. This is not to say he despised doctrine. Of course not. Teaching *is* doctrine. But the Beatitudes are earthed in the everyday. They have unworldly assumptions, it is true. They speak of God, of seeing this God, and a kingdom of Heaven, of being rewarded with a happiness that comes from outside the world. But all the time they talk about living among other people. Nor is it assumed that all the natives are friendly!

It is also important to see that this teaching was originally to a group and not to individuals. When we read the Beatitudes in our Bibles, sitting by ourselves, the setting is, in a sense, bearing false witness. The Beatitudes speak of and assume a corporate way of living. Christ's Christianity is about a new nation, a new family of people living in contrast to the old sort who surround and outnumber them. What Christians have come to be in today's world is more like a number of slightly different individuals caught up in the concerns, customs, and pressures of the society around them. They may have a different set of ideas in their minds, but their group allegiances are to family, neighborhoods, and places of employment, just like everybody else. The busy church is a humming center for many activities and enterprises designed to interest those who hold the Christian arrangement of ideas. All too rarely are they the institutions of a totally new, distinct, and even threatening group within surrounding society.

Few things strike me as more important than that we Christians rediscover our corporate new identity. We are meant to be singled out from the crowds as a group focused on a Master exactly as were those first Galilean believers. And what holds us together and distinguishes us is not our intellectual beliefs (which are far from unimportant) or any particular religious practices (which others can always attend) but our commitment to the Master's life-style. And here again we have what I believe is a subsidiary (but for many, initially, a more real) gospel to that of the cross. Our modern world is a pretty impersonal one. We are tripping over one another in our densely populated towns, cities, estates, and housing areas. We don't seem to count for much in a world full of massive problems and little people. There are two choices—to escape into a dull acceptance of our position as spectators of the world in which we happen to live, or to engage in a meaningful way of life belonging to a group of people who consider themselves our relatives.

The church that Jesus talked about and talked to was meant to be a band of brothers (yes, and sisters!). Anything known as "church" that is not epitomized by this consciousness of being a new family in Jesus and engaged in a particular way of life can never be a setting where people will discover the new happiness of which Jesus spoke.

The rediscovery of this new family consciousness in our churches, however, will probably be a fairly drastic business. It assumes the setting of the Beatitudes—a coming apart from the crowds and the curious to sit at the Master's feet. It assumes that there is in this coming to Jesus a newness that marks believers out from their fellow men (all of whom are equally important to God). Now our present-day Western society churches are rarely willing to go that far, and usually for worthy reasons. There is, first, the fact that we live in a Christianized culture where one has for centuries charitably assumed that at least most of those outside the congregation were in sympathy with Christ and his church. The parish system was built on the assumption that all the inhabitants of each parish were in the same flock and required shepherding rather than capturing (even if relatively few clocked in at the pen on Sunday!). The parable of the wheat and tares told by Jesus should warn us against judging on appearances as to who is the Lord's and who is not. Jesus has always had, and will always have, his secret disciples. Nevertheless, if the charitable assumptions were ever justified they are manifestly inappropriate today. Somehow today's disciples have got to separate themselves from the crowds not in a spirit of rejection and scorn, but out of positive desire to be nearer their Master and their brothers.

On the other hand, the way up the hillside to where the Master's teaching can be heard must never be barred or difficult to climb.

A second reason for the reluctance of churches to be more clearly centers for the new family is that of *evangelism*. We have a gospel to take to the world which means in practice that our churches *should* always have a healthy number of unconvinced fringers. There is an understandable fear of shutting out the seeker. God's people are not meant to be those who put up barriers, freeze people out, or are unconcerned with their fellow men. They are meant to evangelize—to reach out with a good news that can lead to converted lives. So how can we make churches more for insiders without keeping the outsiders out? I suggest that the Beatitudes and their setting give us some clues.

First of all, the disciples set themselves apart from the crowds to concentrate on teaching about living—*but they did not meet in secret.* The picutre I have from Matthew's account is that of Jesus specifically speaking to his followers in the full view of the public (Matt. 7:28 implies that the crowds overheard his teachings). Certainly this was the case frequently throughout the ministry of Jesus. The lines of demarcation were blurred. People could move nearer and were doubtless welcome—but the agenda set by the Master was *specifically* to do with living the distinct life in this world that reflected allegiance to a heavenly authority.

What created the separation between the disciples and the crowds stemmed not from public rejection by the insiders but from the personal attitudes of the outsiders. I believe this is a theme that runs right through the New Testament. Jesus put it starkly when he spoke of not casting pearls before swine. (How the modern press would have made a scandal out of that saying! "Jesus calls nondisciples swine!") Jesus, of course, was not making a judgment of people in those words—rather a statement of fact. People will not respond correctly to what does not interest them. This was why Paul's missionary strategy was never a "cold canvass" of everybody he met. He went to those groups where people's interest coincided or overlapped with his message about a justifying God who could transform lives and who called for a new way of living. Jesus told his disciples on sending them out to preach that they were to go where there was a welcome and to shake even the dust from their feet where they were rejected.

What lies behind all this is that wherever the Master's followers are living out their convictions and sharing their message there is a judgment. But the judgment is meant to be self-imposed. "Light has come into the world, and men loved darkness rather than light," wrote John, as he described his Master's life. It is not for the Christian to impose the judgment on others. The most he can do is go away when he is clearly not wanted (and he shouldn't assume this too readily!). The danger of an overemphasis on evangelism is that it can lead to the Christian or Christian group saying in effect to the crowds, "Keep with us! We'll change our ways somewhat so that you will feel more at home!" This is disastrous. It is not kindness to the unconverted; it is cruelty. The unconverted person has the right to see himself under judgment, *but it must be a judgment that he pronounces upon himself.* If, in spite of a continually warm welcome, a person decides that he does not *belong* to a church, that should not be taken as a case of the church *failing.* It may mean quite the opposite!

The discipleship group, then, is a public one which welcomes any who may come but which discusses and studies (not in some pseudo-academic manner) the business of living in today's world in obedience to Jesus.

27

For those who may still be uneasy about this let me add an important rider. The teaching of the Beatitudes is not about staying in holy huddles but about total involvement in society at large. Christ's people are meant to be fully involved with their fellows in all walks of life. Those of us who believe in the high priority of evangelism should see that it is in this extramural activity of Christ's people that the sharing of the gospel will take place. And I believe it is more likely to be effective because the world will be confronted with "living epistles" rather than apparently abstract or impersonal messages.

And the nearer we are to being living epistles, the nearer we are to discovering the new happiness of which Jesus spoke.

# CHAPTER 3
## *THE TRUTH ABOUT OURSELVES*

The biggest problem we all have to face is the problem of ourselves. At least, that is my experience!

In fact we pose ourselves more than one problem. There is a vast range of inner dilemmas and uncertainties, and most of us never have them all resolved at one and the same time. There is, for example, *the problem of identity*—of working out who we are. Very few of us seem to realize how fruitless it is to try to discover the supposed real self. At certain key times in our lives such as adolescence, adjustment to marriage, the entry into parenthood, seeing one's children leave home, facing retirement, and so on, this problem of identity raises its bewildering head.

Who am I? we continually ask ourselves. Do I really matter? Was what I did yesterday typical of me? Will I make the right impression when I meet So-and-so? And afterward there are those times of despair when we think that we failed to create the impression we intended.

And in all these matters we are not helped by the fact that the answer is, indeed, a complicated one. Our inner dynamics are not static, nor are they simply constructed. There is something within ourselves that is truly of ourselves, individual and constant. But there are additives that make for a bewildering blend. The effects of parental influence, social background, past relationships and traumas are all programmed into us through the years. We are changing creatures. Recently psychiatrists have been suggesting that we never escape from the influence of transactions with our parents in those very early days of our lives when their presences overawed and swamped us. As a result, what really surfaces in us as we react to some situations is the "parent." Again, they say that we never really escape the "child" in ourselves so that we sometimes slip into the emotional reactions of the nursery. Fortunately these psychiatrists recognize that there is the "adult" in us also—the independent-minded, reasoning person (For a popular account see Thomas Harris, *I'm OK, You're OK* [New York: Harper, 1969].) Whether this new school of transactional analysis will prove, in time, to be a mere passing fashion I do not know. A great deal of what they say seems to square with the facts of experience, and much of it is helpful in terms of increasing self-awareness.

But something more than self-awareness is needed. To put an interesting analysis on what our problems seem to be does not always remove them or the distress they can cause. If we are to find a meaningful happiness then we must find something that will hold us together and unify (or at least pacify) the warring factions within ourselves.

Then again there is the *problem of mortality*. The most certain fact of life is that we are all moving toward our deaths. As I mentioned in the first chapter this is one area which we try to put out of our minds for most of the time. But if there is one thing a man cannot do it is to put anything out of his mind. Somehow or other everything stays somewhere!

The result is that we are constantly being made aware of our mortality. Our powers begin to fail. I remember this coming home to me when playing a game with my boys one day when the eldest was about nine or ten years of age. We had to run through some nearby woods to get to a certain point before my wife and daughter, who were taking a shorter route. We started off heartily together, but it was not long before the two small figures of my sons were drawing steadily away from the puffing presence of their father. I began to wish I had never thought of the game!

As we leave youth behind we soon reach a point in our working lives when we have got as far as we are going to get. Ambition and that feeling that the best is yet to come goes, leaving us with less cause to look to the future with any excitement. About the same time our marriages can so easily slip into becoming arrangements. With television to come home to and hobbies or interests to pursue we settle down to whiling away the rest of our lives. A massive entertainment industry is at our disposal; there is much to occupy a mind that would rather avoid asking the awkward questions of old age and death.

31

Any happiness that is to be an improvement on the comfortable pleasantness we can develop in the affluent West has got to meet and conquer the quiet dread of death.

On top of all these problems of the self, the Christian would add *the problem of sin*. In fact it is not an addition. All that we have been considering is evidence of sin. I do not mean by this that our troubled inner dynamics are evidence of personal sin (although they can be at times). What the Bible makes clear and what we so easily overlook is that human sinfulness is far more than the sum total of all the bad things each individual has said, done, or thought. Sin in the Bible is the condition of a species—namely the human race—which was made for fellowship with its Creator and which has broken itself from that one factor which could have held all social, moral, and mental elements in healthy balance.

When the Bible states that the sins of the fathers are passed on to the children to the third and fourth generation, it is merely stating what is inevitable with social creatures. Disorientated humans will breed and raise disorientated humans. Donne was right with his famous words "No man is an island." We are all miniatures of the world, and we are all programmed by the whole of history. Because the world and history are out of true so are we ourselves.

But there is also, of course, the matter of personal sin for which we alone are responsible. A holy God is an awesome prospect, and religious people through ·

the ages have tended either to flog themselves desperately toward a sort of holiness or to sink into despair and inner disgust. Often it has been a mixture of both. Few things can be more destructive of happiness and inner ease than the awareness of the absolute holiness of God that is not balanced with knowledge of his great forgiving love. How, we say to ourselves, can we ever belong within God's sphere of love and power if we disgust him continually?

It is at this point that Jesus began in the Beatitudes "Blessed," he said, "are the poor in spirit, for theirs is the kingdom of heaven." Like all the Beatitudes this stated the very opposite of the obvious. We would surely feel that happiness naturally follows from finding inner prosperity. The word that Jesus used however for poverty is one that implies abject poverty. It is the poverty of the hopeless beggar of his time. How are we to understand what Jesus is saying? Surely there is not comfort in groveling?

The truth is that these words, and what they imply, are the most liberating words a man can hear about himself. The first thing they do is to recognize the truth about the self. We *are* wretched within ourselves. We *are* a tangled mixture of emotions, conflicting personalities, continuous selfishness, and more. We spend a great deal of time covering up for this and running away from the reality. What Jesus does straight away is to say that personal happiness comes from recognizing the truth about ourselves and realizing that our heavenly Father is happy for us to belong to him *exactly as we are*. The issue is not whether God *approves*. It is whether God *accepts*. And he does. "Theirs is the kingdom of heaven," is what Jesus said.

It is amazing how easily this truth gets forgotten. Religious people have continually slipped into trying to build up some spiritual "wealth" in order to "maintain" acceptance. The result can only be disappointment, or the catastrophe of believing in a God whose standards of holiness have been brought down to earth. Neither result brings much assurance—because it can only be bought at the cost of self-deception, and ultimately self-deception is an impossibility. The truth will come to the surface sooner or later.

A common mistake is to say that this idea of recognizing one's spiritual poverty only refers to *becoming* a Christian. We come as beggars, but he gives us the resources to become Lords. It sounds very attractive. We start as defeated people in the matter of righteousness (which is true) and God in his mercy accepts us that way (which is also true), but then with his help we go on to the possibility of becoming victors. This last thought—while it seems to be supported by such verses as Paul claiming that we are "more than conquerors through him who loved us"—is a dangerously misleading one. Jesus did not say, "Blessed are those who once were spiritually poor." He said literally, "Blessed ones are the spiritually poor ones." He assumed the condition of inner poverty would remain constant.

34

Paul makes this very point throughout the early chapters of Romans. He is well aware of what his critics would say. In fact he voices the criticism on their behalf: "Are we to continue in sin that grace may abound?" (Rom. 6:1). Or again, "Are we to sin because we are not under law but under grace?" (Rom. 6:15). Paul's reply is to point out that no one who has experienced God's wonderful forgiveness could set out *deliberately to make a policy of sinning* so that God can grant even more forgiveness. Acceptance by God is not a liberation from God's standards of behavior, but it is a liberation from despair and remorse when we realize that—for all our best intentions—we often have fallen below those standards. The truth is that we *do* continue to sin and that God's grace *does* continue to abound.

Of course people do become better people when they follow Christ. We can all see this. Sometimes we see quite startling changes for the better in other people. My experience is, however, that the person who is seen to be improving is usually the last to realize this. The more one grows aware of the nearness of Christ the more one becomes aware of one's own inner poverty. 1904049

I have heard many sermons on the subject of "victorious Christian living." I am sure that there are books and pamphlets galore on the subject. But the truth is that words like "victory" and "conquering" are never used in the Bible to refer to the spiritual achievements of an individual Christian.

I believe it is necessary to stress this because I have

35

found so many Christians who have been despondent about lack of victory in their lives. Very subtly, wanting to be better Christians for the Lord's sake has become wanting to be better so as to "remain" in God's favor. Nothing could be more unnecessary.

The victory the Bible talks about is Christ's victory, and it is a total victory over this problem of continuing sin. This is what Paul is saying when he relates his own experiences in the seventh chapter of Romans. One is left at the end of that chapter without any evidence of Paul having gained a victory over the fact that when he wants "to do right, evil lies close at hand" (Rom. 7:21). Rather one is left with the amazing realization that the battle has never been significant to God because he refuses to condemn! The opening words of the eighth chapter make clear that all the condemnation for our *continuing* sin has been dealt with in Jesus Christ's life and death for us.

We will always be spiritual paupers in God's sight; nevertheless we will always be accepted and belong within his plans and his kingdom. The recognition of this brings a great release from the sense of guilt and self-doubt. Here is the source of a new happiness indeed. We can look at ourselves and say, "Yes, I am a pretty poor specimen but God loves me in spite of it all, and he has taken me into his kingdom knowing that I may never become much better!"

In all this talk about recognizing the truth of our spiritual poverty there is one danger to avoid. The liberation this Beatitude brings stems not from the fact that we are poor in spirit *but from the fact that God expects no more.* Every now and again I have met someone who has believed it right to dwell on his or her unworthiness almost to the exclusion of rejoicing in God's continuing accepting kindness. This can lead to terrible depression and can cripple the spirit rather than set it free. Introspection is like some poisonous drugs. Used under doctor's orders in small doses they stimulate and improve health. Used in large doses they destroy.

This, however, might be thought to have little relevance to the matters of identity, mortality, and our mixed-up inner dynamics; but it has. I am not saying that an insight into the first Beatitude provides a cure for depression. What I am saying is that it is sound therapy to ponder over its meaning. What my real self is, matters little. God accepts me as I am, and his opinion is the only one that counts. If I must keep suspecting that people are against me the one person who is constantly *for* me is Almighty God. If my inner dynamics are of the type that makes me want to fight to get attention and makes me overanxious for affection from those around, then the message of the first Beatitude applies to me also. It says, even at my worst, I am accepted by God and favored by him. It goes further. It says that God's favor is far more than passing, kindly feeling. It says that I am actually fitted into God's plans—part of his team; for this is the meaning of the words "for theirs is the kingdom of heaven." I *belong.*

So the battle for acceptance by God is unnecessary. Like the father in the parable of the prodigal son, he runs to meet the failure who comes dejectedly home. And the battle to remain in God's favor is unnecessary also. We are accepted by the King with parts to play in his plans. We can save up all our nervous energy and ambitions for the work he wants us to do, because the issue of our own acceptibility is beyond doubt.

This is the liberating secret of the new happiness. The dread of death has less of a hold upon a man or woman who realizes he is safe in the hands of the eternal God. The man who is in a tangle over working out *who* he really is has the assurance that God knows the answer. As the days unfold he will reveal the tasks and role in life that fit the real self. And all the time we must remember that we are not talking about the private affairs of a Christian. We saw in the previous chapter that the Beatitudes were given by Jesus to a group of people who had chosen to follow him. True Christian fellowship is one of mutual support. It is based on an understanding that every one of the members is a highly imperfect person. This recognition of common need is the finest basis one could ask for in a supportive, healing community. So many of our psychological difficulties stem from our loneliness and sense of isolation from those around us. The group of "sinners anonymous" that Jesus assumed in his Beatitudes should be a setting where we can better cope with ourselves and other selves. When we crack and the stresses show, the Christian is meant to be surrounded by the best help possible—his understanding, brotherly friends.

Finally we must note that the first Beatitude is followed by the others. The poor-spirited individual is surrounded by his fellows and called to a life of involvement in a world that is full of need. So one is given purpose and set goals to pursue. These again are health-giving factors for a troubled mind.

Yet for many today, all this is theory, and the reality at local church level is something very different. Often one is tempted to soldier on with a sort of private religion due to the fact that the official churches are so impersonal. Far from being accepting, purposeful communities, they have become gatherings of Christ-believing but self-protecting individuals. It is difficult to know which is more tragic: the fact that the world does not see real Christian community, or the fact that very few Christians ever experience it. The packed suburban church building with its large choir and its jammed parking lot has about as much in common with a group of mutually supportive spiritual paupers as a football crowd in the local stadium. Fortunately we are beginning to see this, and one of the most encouraging developments in modern church life is the widespread development with churches of small groups where we can really get alongside one another.

# CHAPTER 4
## *THE TRUTH ABOUT OUR WORLD*

The Beatitudes talk about the same world as my daily newspaper. Consider what lies behind such phrases as: *blessed are those who mourn; blessed are those who hunger and thirst for righteousness; blessed are the merciful; blessed are the peacemakers; blessed are those who are persecuted.*

In a perfectly satisfactory world none of these phrases would make any sense. There would be nothing to mourn, no missing righteousness to hunger after, no need to be merciful, no peace to be made, and nobody being persecuted. Jesus set the happiness he talked about not only against the background of personal shortcomings but also in the center of a highly unsatisfactory world.

But he did more. He claimed that happiness came from involvement in this unsatisfactory world. So many of our notions of happiness are summed up in the phrase about "getting away from it all." Jesus said directly the opposite. Happiness is found when we go headfirst into it all. The problem is that practically none of us acts as though we really believed this!

We Christians look at our contemporaries and see

such things as the boom in packaged holidays, the multiplicity of fantasy-producing literature, the non stop television watching, the huge sales of alcohol and consumption of tobacco, the swamping audio-blanket of pop, the growing resort to drugs, the worship of sport, the compulsion to buy goods almost for the sake of acquisition—and we shake our heads gravely. Escapism has become heavy industry. Unfortunately our solemn thoughts about the folly of most of these matters do not penetrate into our own self-awareness. We are ourselves caught up frequently in the passion for diversion that is all around us. Not only that, but we have evolved our own forms of diversion also. Indeed this whole matter of religious escapism is one that needs more attention than it is getting.

Christians in the West, and in particular those of my own Bible-believing evangelical variety, have managed to surround themselves with their own unreal culture. We have our own entertainers in the popular speakers, preachers, platform personalities, and gospel musicians. We are writing our own Christian musicals and raising up our own Christian poets and writers. None of these things, when viewed individually, is in any sense undesirable. But what happens when all these human ingredients and their outputs are brought together is that we have the mixture for a pie of pure escapism.

In 1973 a British gospel folk pair known as Ishmael and Andy gave up their musical ministry. A pleasant and sincere young couple, they had reached the conclusion that they were becoming little more than entertainers for Christians. In my own world of publishing what has happened is that in America and Britain a huge outpouring of literature is going into the captive markets of church congregations through bookstores and church bookstalls. Through the religious journals, continuous advertising and commendation is motivating remarkable sales. This in turn has alerted publishers to find more and more manuscripts that will appeal to the captive market almost regardless of their ultimate value. The vision that took many of us into the field of Christian literature has been a hard one to keep unsullied. The church, of course, needs reading material to help it face and challenge the world. The danger from a surfeit of popular religious literature is that it will be too absorbed to face the world at all.

The same dynamics which make Christian communication inward rather than outgoing can be seen in popular big-congregation preaching on the one hand and the incessant round of conferences and conventions on the other. These can so easily be diversions, time-consumers, and escape routes for Christian activity. They need not be; they should not be; they often are. Once again, the acid test of their worth is whether they help us to face the harsh world outside or whether they encourage us to avoid it.

One of the most publicized developments of recent years in the Christian world is the charismatic movement. This movement is concerned to emphasize the need for Christians to exercise the gifts of

the Spirit as recorded in the New Testament—
especially in the Corinthian epistles. Thus there is
renewed interest in speaking in tongues, interpretation of tongues, prophecy, healing, and so on. It is
impossible to deny that the New Testament speaks of
these matters. It is certainly true that our modern
churches need the breath of spiritual revival, and I
for one believe that God is bringing this to many
congregations through the charismatic movement.

Nevertheless I have observed a disturbing factor
about this movement *in practice*. This is that it has
created an almost totally absorbing mini-world for its
adherents. They have spawned their own breed of
books. They seem to have engendered a considerable
number of conferences, conventions, special services, and small group meetings. They have their
own magazines, their own personalities, their own
approved four-star churches to which many will
travel long distances on Sundays. In short, they are
in danger of organizing themselves out of being
citizens of the same world as their neighbors.

Of course all this is merely a larger scaled version
of what many of us are doing to ourselves in our own
round of local church activities. It is so easy, and
pleasant, to tie up large amounts of time in close
company with other Christians, and we can find
impressive-sounding reasons for doing so. There is
an episode during Christ's ministry which we
preachers are fond of using to illustrate this pressure
to cling to the precious. It concerns the occasion
when Jesus took Peter, James, and John up "a high

mountain apart" and they saw him transfigured. Peter's reaction was to say, "It is well that we are here," and to want to build shelter for an extended stay. Jesus however led them back down from their mountaintop experience, and within a few verses we read that they returned to the crowd and were confronted with a distraught father and his epileptic son. The moral is clear—we cannot stay on our blessed mountaintops. We have to return and live in the real world where there is suffering and where there are problems.

The Beatitudes were about happiness, but they were not about escapism. Jesus told his followers that they would face mourning, agonizing over wrongs in the world, the need to be merciful, and the probability of opposition. There is very little "getting away from it all" in these things.

What did Jesus mean by "mourning"? One way of finding out is to see in what ways he could be described as having mourned himself. One well known incident is at the death of Lazarus (John 11). This is an interesting passage because it is clear that Jesus knows that Lazarus will be dead when he arrives at the village of Bethany and he also knows that he is going to awake him out of sleep (v. 11). And yet when Jesus actually finds himself among those who are mourning Lazarus' death he breaks down and weeps (v. 35). We are not told why he loses his composure but we know it cannot be that Lazarus is "dead and gone" in Jesus' understanding. The truth would appear to be that Jesus shared the human misery of that situation. He did not allow himself to be detached.

Jesus is described as weeping on another occasion. In Luke's account of his triumphal entry into Jerusalem we learn that "when he drew near and saw the city he wept over it, saying, 'Would that even today you knew the things that make for peace'" (Luke 19:42). From his further remarks it is clear that he could foresee future conquest of the beloved Jerusalem. Both his act of weeping and the cause came over as very Jewish. He entered into the aspirations of his people. He not only became a man, he became a Jew; fully entering into the feel of his proud but oppressed nation.

There are many other instances where we read of a Jesus whose feelings could be overwhelming. The word "compassion" is used in English translations on several occasions referring to Christ's feelings. It is, literally, a gutless translation of the word the New Testament writers used to describe feelings that went down to one's very bowels. Another relevant factor is the description of Jesus' extreme exhaustion at times. The Jesus who could sleep in a small boat during a storm was clearly someone who had given out everything he had both physically and emotionally.

The prophet Isaiah had foreseen "a man of sorrows, and acquainted with grief" who would be uniquely God's servant. Peter clearly, in his own writing, identified the prophet's suffering servant with Jesus. The fact that he did so identify Jesus could only have been because Jesus fitted the description—he was indeed a man of sorrows and acquainted with grief. But whose sorrows and grief? Certainly the betrayal, arrest, trial, and crucifixion were appalling moments. But until that week he had enjoyed good health and had moved around almost unmolested.

The grief and sorrow that Peter saw was, I suggest, more than that of his own passion. It was total immersion into the cares of a sick society whose sickness was bound to lead to his own rejection and destruction.

Yet Jesus could not be described as a miserable person or even as a sad person. He entered fully into the cares of people but doubtless into their joys as well. Perhaps Paul was reflecting the spirit of his Master particularly well when he wrote on one occasion, "Who is weak, and I am not weak?" (II Cor. 11:29) and another, "Rejoice with those who rejoice, weep with those who weep" (Rom. 12:15).

Today it seems we are afraid of emotions. We have honored the concept of the "cool" man who calmly takes both fortune and misfortune in his stride. Indeed it is hard to deny that this not giving way to emotions is a fine, mature quality. Yet Jesus could not be described as giving way to his emotions. His feelings did not rule his life or determine his policies. If they had he would never have stayed in the garden to await his betrayer. No, the truth is that he was a *total* man and that very few of us approximate his totality. His emotions were not suppressed, but neither did they dominate. Rather they led to the considered action of a man who was totally absorbed. He was not cool—he was *warm*.

It is this warmth that is so often lacking in human relationships today. One of the disturbing developments in public behavior in recent years is *affectlessness*. People are becoming less affected by what goes on around them. In no sense do we feel that we are our brother's keepers. In recent years there have been several reports of murders and muggings in public places where people observed but made no attempt to interfere. One of the most quoted is that of the murder in New York of Kitty Genovese. It took place in public and people saw it happening. Nobody tried to intervene. Nobody even telephoned the police.

There are various theories as to why affectlessness is developing. Some blame it on television and the development of a sort of spectator mentality. Others see a trend in densely populated conditions for people to turn in on themselves and to try to lock out the bewilderment of reality. Paul Simon's song "I Am a Rock" expresses this perfectly. The song speaks of trying to keep out practically every emotion in an attempt to avoid getting hurt. "If I'd never loved I never would have cried," the singer complains.

And of course the words are true. Love—unselfish concern for another—can and does bring pain. It brought a cross to Jesus. And the Christian is told that the pattern of the cross is the pattern of all true love. But there is another cause of affectlessness that we would do well to remember. That is busyness and

47

overcrowded time. For some reason Christians have been persuaded that the crowded diary, the busy schedule is an obvious virtue. It is nothing of the sort. It might well be that the Priest and Levite in the Good Samaritan story were hurrying to their ecclesiastical engagements. I certainly remember trying to persuade a drunk man in London, whose cut eye was bleeding badly, to come to a hospital with me. All the time I was conscious that I was making myself late for a speaking engagement, and I almost breathed a sigh of relief when he insisted on staying where he was, reeking of urine and alcohol. I'm none too proud of that memory.

Many a child of a Christian home has suffered because one or both of the parents was too busy "in the cause of Christ"—too busy to be a proper father or mother to what was, thereby, a deprived child! Many a congregation has generated such a round of activities, training programs, committees and subcommittees that it has not given its members time to look at or live in the same world as their neighbors. Whether our Christian affectlessness stems from some social sickness, hardness of heart, or over busyness—the result is the same. We don't *appear* to care, and those who need our outgoing love do not receive it.

Caring, of course, involves action. The Beatitudes are not merely talking about *feelings* when they refer to mourning, being merciful, hungering and thirsting after righteousness, and so on. It is here we have to note that sentiment is not enough. There are some

48

very poignant protest songs being sung by suitably sincere looking, and sounding, singers. But a song changes nothing. I sometimes wonder whether those who sing such songs as "Blowing in the Wind" think that by so doing they are changing anything in the unjust world of which the song speaks. The truth is, of course, that they are not. Further, if the singing of such songs becomes a substitute for action then the songs are a diversion from reality and, in practice, are self-contradictory. Again, a missionary hymn doesn't send out a missionary, and if our missionary interests are totally enveloped in a world of raising funds, singing moving hymns, and reading missionary magazines then the missionary cause is little advanced.

The Old Testament tells us the story of Nehemiah. In the first chapter of the book, Nehemiah learns that the walls and gates of Jerusalem have fallen into serious disrepair. As an exile from that land he could be excused for feeling that it was no longer a matter for his concern, but that was not how he viewed it. His reaction was first to weep, then to pray, and finally to seek a way to act.

The Christian response to an imperfect and often tragic world is one that calls for mourning and for the desire to act—"Blessed are those who hunger and thirst for righteousness." Yet I fear that we are frequently wide of such a response.

The first reason for this is that not only does our religious busyness keep us too preoccupied to notice some of the surrounding suffering, but that many

Christians feel it is not right to be anything other than joyful. This is a frequent product of some types of Christian teaching. The great goal we set ourselves is to be triumphant, rejoicing Christians and therefore any solemnity or sadness is letting down the side. We need to see how false, indeed how callous, this pseudo-spirituality is. Jesus wept and so may we! Joy does not mean the same as joviality.

The second reason for our lack of concern is that we tend to intellectualize the concern so that it doesn't lead to pain, let alone action. This is done by *discussion*. The world must have been put right a million times over by Christians clustered around their coffee cups; but the stock of righteousness is not advanced one jot in fact. What is needed is to move from discussion of big issues into participation in smaller, more mundane needs that are at hand.

The Beatitudes speak of a jagged, painful world and a response to it that allows the barbs to enter one's own soul. Yet all this is not incompatible with happiness. The reason for this is simple. To open oneself concernedly and vulnerably to the real world is to do what Jesus did. And to take the path that he took is to draw deeply on the Holy Spirit that he possessed. God is still—I'm glad to say—concerned for his world. To share his concerns is to find oneself close to the heart of Almighty God—and that is what leads to the new happiness.

# CHAPTER 5
## *ACHIEVEMENT WITHOUT AGGRESSION*

As I walked up the concourse in Dallas airport toward the security checkpoint I was struck by a large notice ahead of me. I read:

COMMENTS REGARDING GUNS AND BOMBS ARE TAKEN SERIOUSLY. PLEASE, NO JOKES!

Somehow that notice has stuck in my mind ever since. It was saying two things at least—first that aggression is no laughing matter and second, that aggression is a reality in everyday life. The security procedures at an airport are now accepted as part of life. It is almost not news any more when an airliner, its passengers, and crew are held for ransom on account of some political cause or private pocket. People take to sky-jacking because they believe that it is an effective way of achieving some objective. The power to destroy is the key to attainment—so they think.

And, quite frankly, most of us agree with the air pirates! By this I mean that we see power—the power to destroy obstacles in our path—as the way to getting things done. The most obvious examples of this outlook in our modern world belong to the activities of guerrilla forces, call "freedom fighters" by those who agree with their causes or "terrorists" by those who do not. The whole fabric of life on our planet is being threatened today more by the ability of minorities to wreak havoc on majorities than by the readiness of large nations to declare war upon each other. It seems also that the modern mind has decided that the *scale* of aggression has got to be altered if political and social changes are to be achieved. The modern mind does not appear to have seriously examined whether *aggression itself* should be abandoned as the means towards attainment.

And yet a horrifying world war is within living memory to stand as an object lesson for us all. Adolf Hitler succeeded in mesmerizing a noble, ingenious, and industrious nation. By a naked psychological assault upon sensibility and judgment he succeeded, where no one else had succeeded, in brainwashing an entire nation. From this achievement he mobilized for a physical assault upon his neighboring states, and the initial results of the jackbooted military hordes was horrific and impressive. At the end of 1940 one could write this commentary upon history:

BLESSED ARE THE AGGRESSIVE FOR THEY SHALL OVERWHELM THE EARTH.

But by the end of 1940 the full story had not been told.

## ACHIEVEMENT WITHOUT AGGRESSION

Now we can look back. Hitler's Third Reich is a bad memory despised by all men, including most Germans. The massive aggression mounted by Nazism only succeeded in achieving an even more massive counter-aggression, and the suffering brought to the people of Germany was immense, as their fighting men were slain, their conquests reversed, their cities scorched, and their proud country politically carved in two—perhaps for all time. I do not say that the message of such history is that meekness destroys aggression. I suggest it is that *aggression does not ultimately achieve very much.*

When Jesus said, "Blessed are the meek, for they shall inherit the earth," he was not only indicating a way we should live, he was also making an observation on history. It is an observation that we could and should be making for ourselves if only we had eyes to see. His words suggest to me an allusion to the achievements of Moses. The ancient Hebrew leader is described in the book of Numbers as "very meek, more than all men that were on the face of the earth" (Num. 12:3), and yet Moses led a whole nation of slaves into the possession of their own territory. Moses could never be described as a weak man. He held a frightened rabble together, gave them identity, formulated and administered their laws under divine guidance, and wrote a historical saga of the whole story.

Yet it is important to see that this man of resourcefulness, privileged upbringing, and magnetic leadership went to the Pharaoh, who controlled the destiny of the enslaved Israelites, not to threaten or to declare hostilities but simply to *ask* him again and again to "let my people go."

It is true that the events that led to the release of the children of Israel and to their successful escape from pursuing Egyptian armies contained violence and destruction. But none of this issued from the aggression of Moses—it came as a result of the intervention of Almighty God.

When Jesus exhalted meekness, he was of course advocating one of the clearest hallmarks of his own life-style. The temptations in the wilderness were about how he could achieve his objectives as the unique Son of the world's Father-Creator. In one way or another those temptations were about the use and abuse of power. And we who live in the latter half of the twentieth century should study those temptations closely, for the use and abuse of power is *our* dilemma above all others. The conclusion at which Jesus arrived was that right objectives must have right means. If one's objective is for the enhancing of people, one's endeavors to achieve that objective must not destroy or manipulate the very same people.

So Jesus rejected aggressive power, although the episode in cleansing the temple revealed that he could always have exercised that option. The fact that Jesus only used physical violence on one occasion is far less puzzling than the fact that he did not use it more often when one notes how effective it was. The temple episode, however, reveals all the marks of a

54

deliberately staged, enacted parable well known to students of the Hebrew prophets. I very much doubt if any man was physically hurt, but I have no doubts that they ran for their very lives!

In physical terms Jesus was overpowered. Men took him by force in the Garden of Gethsemane. Men marched him to a hastily arranged trial. Men with the power of life and death passed Jesus to each other to pass judgment. Crowds chanted for his destruction and overpowered the wavering military governor. Soldiers flogged him, stripped him, hammering his living flesh onto wooden spars, and hung him up to die. The meekness of Jesus did not defeat the aggression of his executioners. And yet who now would praise or even note the achievements of those who killed Christ? Even those of differing faiths, or no faith at all, would agree that at least at the level of integrity, nobility, example, and the ability to call forth admiration, the achievement on Good Friday rests with the man who died.

But when they took the shattered body of Jesus from the cross the full story had not yet been told. The whole history of Christianity stems not from a dead hero but from an amazing demonstration of otherworldly power. Jesus was raised from the dead. In exactly the same manner as we have seen with Moses, the man who disavowed aggression in the cause of what was right was vindicated and *given* victorious achievement.

One of the more fashionable interpretations of the atonement in recent years centers around a helpful

thought. This is that Jesus absorbed all the hurtful-
ness and cruelty of men without retaliation. A hurtful
and sinful act is like a pebble thrown into water. Not
only is there a disturbance at the point of entry, there
are outgoing ripples of disturbance afterward. With
the cross, and the cry of "Father forgive them"
covering his executioners, Jesus set up no "ripples."
Evil was absorbed and removed.

As a complete explanation of the meaning of the
cross this is quite inadequate, but as a description of
one aspect of Jesus' life and death it is tremendously
illuminating. Here is a model for living in an evil
world.

Jesus expounded this theme in the Sermon on the
Mount:

> You have heard that it was said, "An eye for an eye
> and a tooth for a tooth." But I say to you, Do not resist
> one who is evil. But if any one strikes you on the right
> cheek, turn to him the other also. (Matt. 5:38-39)

No one could claim that the meekness of Jesus was,
in fact, weakness. To be gentle in a vicious world
calls for a greater courage than is required for
anything else. When Jesus was arrested in the
Garden, Peter drew a sword against all the odds and
was clearly brave enough to die in the duel of
aggression and counter-aggression. When later Peter
was challenged outside the courtroom and could
possibly have joined his master on a scaffold, he had
not the courage to declare his loyalty. He was brave
enough to die sword in hand, but he was not brave

enough to die with a nail through his palm. Most of us are like that. Aggression dulls our awareness of the pain we receive and the pain we inflict. Meekness heightens our awareness on both counts.

It is, perhaps, almost inexplicable that so few people in history have tried to develop a politics of meekness, for the achievements of Moses and Jesus are far from unique. Secular history has many instances where not only has aggression been shown to be counter-productive but where people pursuing their ends with gentleness have triumphed. Perhaps Gandhi is the supreme example of a man who developed a politics of gentleness, although it is a moot point whether he was influenced by the example of Jesus in this respect. Gandhi in seeking to unite and lead a colonized nation taught the ways of *ahimsa* (loving nonviolence) and *tapasya* (readiness to suffer on behalf of others). Two things followed—we might also say inevitably. First Gandhi was murdered. Second, India achieved its independence.

Today Gandhi would be viewed as a symbol of the political way forward by many people—particularly those of the younger generations. I fear, however, that the tactics of peaceful protest and demonstration with which we are so familiar nowadays are a distortion of Gandhi's teaching. We are certainly seeing a distortion of Jesus Christ's meekness. What so frequently happens now is that the aggression is moved from the physical plane to the psychological. So often in modern mass demonstrations a careful and irresistible manipulation takes place to incite violence against those who demonstrate. Thus we have a manipulated martyrdom which is meant to distort the true facts. Those vested with the unenviable task of maintaining order are provoked into trying to achieve this end by resorting to force, and the ever-present television camera records the images of police or military brutality. The fact that the demonstrators in some cases have psychologically manipulated the aggression that has come upon them, and done it for public relations purposes, is something that no camera lens could ever discern.

Thus the hope that the principle of meekness might become an effective means of achieving political progress is now a thin one. We have polluted the concept, and the reason is simple to see. Meekness is more than a technology for achieving ends. It is a manifestation of love and unselfishness. All the virtues of Christ depend upon one another.

At this point therefore we must look away from issues and turn our gaze upon ourselves. All that I have said thus far is the stuff of which detached religious discussions are made. When Jesus first pronounced the Beatitudes he was doing more than making general observations about life. He was planting the seeds of a way of life into the minds and hearts of his followers. If I claim to be a follower of Jesus, the Beatitudes are for me! I am meant to be living my life with these objectives and considerations in mind. Meekness is my business even if the rest of the world should reject it as impracticable. Christians are meant to be God's gentle people.

## ACHIEVEMENT WITHOUT AGGRESSION

This requires seeing what in us and around us is evidence of aggressiveness rather than meekness—and there is plenty to see. It requires living out a life of gentleness as a witness to the very nature of our Lord himself. When I look at myself I see a considerable amount of latent anger, thrustfulness, venom, and love of destruction. Yet, because I have been brought up as a respectable middle-class citizen I can also see that I have a fairly thick veneer of politeness and dislike of unpleasantness on the top. What being a Christian has done for me is that the veneer is perhaps thicker and might fool some onlooker into thinking that what he sees is the truth at all levels of the personality. Alas, the truth is otherwise.

I have noticed how I can come home from situations where my patience has held up under great pressure only to crack at the first frustration within the family. I've roared at my bewildered children, overreacted and snapped at my wife, and only failed to kick the cat because of its ability to move at something approaching the speed of light! Many a red patch on a naughty child's rump was probably received vicariously! I'm sure this is true in our family, and I can only hope that the children will learn to forgive me as well as they have learned to keep out of range at the wrong times! The fact of the matter is that we all have inner aggressions trying to get out, and get out they must. So what do we do about it?

Certainly we do nothing but harm if we try to deny this fact because we are "new people in Christ"! All of us can think of preachers who make sweeping assertions about the meaning of the new creation that takes place with regard to the man who is "in Christ." Such preachers can so easily make us wonder whether we are Christians at all. The way they talk would seem to imply that they themselves have found total liberation from all those undesirable inner flaws that mark the lives of the rest of us. The truth is otherwise. I mix with preachers practically every day, and they are the salt of the earth. They are also amply endowed with such qualities as irritability, pride, selfishness, and a lot more besides. When they are preaching on the appropriate subject they (like Paul of old) are prepared to admit that sin dwells within. Unfortunately when they are preaching on holiness they can so easily make statements that imply something different. Holiness is a goal to aim at but it is not meant to be a stick to beat us into the ground.

As a preacher myself I know how easy it is to wield that discouraging stick. Again I must ask—what do I do about the inner aggressions? Do I settle for the thicker veneer? Is there nothing more?

Certainly I believe there is more. Paul could speak both of sin dwelling within *and also of Christ dwelling within* (Rom. 7:18). The veneer is no longer telling a lie. For the Christian it tells a partial truth. Beneath the surface and into the mysterious depths of our soul the new nature of Christ is battling with the old nature. Becoming a Christian usually creates a conflict that was not in existence before. The man who has never encountered the holy nature of Jesus is likely to be more at ease about his inner wickedness and spiritual poverty. He might even be totally unaware of it. For the Christian, awareness and dissatisfaction are heightened because he has glimpsed perfection. So what can he do?

The first thing he does is to "put on" the Christian qualities of love and gentleness. The words "put on" (Col. 3:12 ff.) are not mine. They belong to Paul, the supreme teacher in the New Testament of the idea of newness in Christ. Whatever having the indwelling Christ means and whatever he intended us to understand by the idea of being a new creation, he still called for us to make conscious efforts with regard to Christian virtues. And coupled to these positive, conscious efforts he linked the idea of conscious attempts to eradicate or "put to death" such "earthly" factors as "anger, wrath, malice, slander and foul talk" (Col. 3:8). Now the question must be asked about all this—in what way is this any different from hypocrisy? Is not this "putting on" merely the putting on of an act?

The answer to this question is yes! It *is* putting on an act. But it is an act that the Christian is equipped to play. The Holy Spirit can develop his fruits in our lives if we want this to happen. But the only way we can show that we want the fruits of the Spirit is to attempt to put on the qualities of Christ. We are not meant to sit around, do nothing, and expect the fruits of the Spirit to sprout out of our ears. Sometimes we talk as if this should happen, but most of the proof texts for such a view come from Paul, and he clearly did not believe such a proposition.

Having said all this, however, we are still left with the problem of those residual aggressions fighting to get out. Does putting them to death mean that we pretend they don't exist? I think not. It means that we dispose of them in an area where they cannot harm anybody, not even the cat! There is only one way to do that, and it is a way that relatively few Christians seem to have realized. We are meant to pour out our anger *toward God himself!* This is what David did. It is what Jeremiah did. There is abundant evidence of it in the Bible, and yet so many of us feel that our prayers should always be processed into a religious type of politeness.

I confess that I rarely have the good sense to follow the example of King David. If I have been involved in a painful clash with someone where I have returned soft answers to constant abuse, the likelihood is that next time I have the car to myself I shall spit the real feelings on my mind toward the windscreen wipers. This is certainly better than doing it toward the person in question, but the problem is that it tends only to reinforce the resentment I feel at being abused. No—the true way is to tell God exactly what I feel. He knows anyway! If I feel that God shouldn't have allowed me to be so treated I might as well say it and have the relief from getting it out of my system. He is already aware that I feel that way so I might as well be honest.

Things like a hard dig in the garden (one of my

wife's great ploys) or a vigorous walk all help—but to let it all come out before our understanding and unshockable Heavenly Father is still the best way.

At this point it would be useful to consider an apparent contradiction. Jesus was meek and called us to be the same, and yet the Bible is not short of references to the notion of having power in our lives. Indeed there are four different Greek words in the New Testament reflecting some facet of the nature of power. Many Christians today are searching for more power in their Christian witness. How is this to be reconciled with the call to live gentle lives?

The answer is that power belongs to God. The Christian draws on the power of God, but he cannot at random release it. There is a very big difference between the Christian meekly relying on a powerful God and the magician developing ways to manipulate and channel supernatural power. Stephen is described as a man "full of grace and power" (Acts 6:8) who "did great wonders and signs among the people." When, however, men set out to stone him to death he died just as anyone else would have done in the circumstances. There was no divine provision of a force field to keep the stones away. There was no miraculous intervention. The power of God was present in a less dramatic form. Stephen was given the strength to forgive his murderers.

The wilderness temptations of Jesus showed that he ruled out any notion of expecting a supernaturally protected life. He was, if anything, a very reluctant miracle worker, and his powers were never used to bend men's minds or afflict their bodies. Jesus so respected the self-will of others that he let himself be crucified because that was what his contemporaries wanted to do with him. It is important that we do not expect God to deal differently with us. That God can and does act powerfully and supernaturally through us from time to time is a fact, but we are not meant to be the spiritual equivalents of Batman. The model for God's power in the experience of the meek man is the death and resurrection of Christ. If we want to have the power of his resurrection we must be prepared to face the agony of his crucifixion. To pretend otherwise is to retreat from the reality of the Bible and the world into the fool's paradise.

So far I have been discussing Christian gentleness with regard to human relationships. I believe we are meant to take meekness further into every part of our lives. Aggressiveness is a hallmark of our industrialized society. The call to lead a gentle life challenges aggressive cars, clothes, attitudes to sex, sports, politics, and much else. Christians need to witness to the gentleness of Jesus, and I believe our society today desperately needs this witness. We have practically all been brainwashed into believing that happiness is related to packing as many events and happenings into our lives as possible and becoming more involved with things rather than people. Thus the much talked about energy crisis is seen as an appalling threat to happiness and civilization.

The fact is that greater use of our feet or a pair of

bicycle wheels would enhance most of our lives. More time sitting reflecting on life and savoring relationships with people, animals, and nature would increase the intensity of our happiness. I believe that a distinctive prophetic hallmark of Christians today should be that their life-style reveals a slowing down of the pace of life and the development of gentler interests and activities. One of my outstanding memories from a trip to the United States was of seeing Amish farmers in Pennsylvania. These people have tried to maintain the life-style they had when they first came to America from Germany two hundred years ago. They wear the same plain clothes. They eat the same plain foods. They have held out against the automobile and electricity and still plow with mules. Less extreme groups such as the plain people Mennonites are perhaps more impressive. They have taken what can be enhancing from technology and yet have refused to sell out to a great deal of the rat race of fashion and social custom. I shall never forget meeting these people in the Farmer's Market at Lancaster where they sold their homemade wares and quietly indicted the impersonality of the super-market. I felt the poorer for being on the outside of their way of life.

Paul wrote:

Have this mind among yourselves, which is yours in Christ Jesus, who, though he was in the form of God, did not count equality with God a thing to be grasped, but emptied himself, taking the form of a servant, being born in the likeness of men. And being found in human form he humbled himself and became obedient unto death, even death on a cross. Therefore God has highly exalted him . . . (Phil. 2:5-9).

What these words do is to sketch out the dynamics of Christ's self-imposed meekness and to highlight the way in which, through the Father's intervention, meekness is rewarded with attainment. Paul wrote these words to a squabbling church. The Philippian Christians had their internal rivalries—like so many Christian groups. Paul's intention was that his readers should see in the pattern of Christ's own life-style a way forward for themselves. It has to start in the mind and in the outlook on life. It is no use criticizing church support for guerrilla forces in Africa if we are engaging in aggressive policies on the church council or using techniques of evangelism that try to pressure people into Christian faith. We are all called to look upon ourselves as servants of God and of our fellow men. We are all called to face the possibility of our own crucifixions.

The world around us knows very little about meekness. If Christians can only learn to put on this quality both corporately and in personal lives something precious will be brought into our frayed civilization. For us as Christians the path of meekness can only bring a profound happiness. There will be the happiness of breaking free from the rat race. But more than this, there will be the joy of finding the power of the Holy Spirit to equip us for the task of imitating the very life-style of Jesus himself.

# CHAPTER 6
## *RIGHT IS MIGHT*

The clearest proof that Jesus did not equate meekness with weakness in the Beatitudes is to be found in the words that immediately followed:

> Blessed are those who hunger and thirst for righteousness, for they shall be satisfied.

The juxtaposition of these two statements is masterly. Meekness without a driving concern for righteousness can only become something insipid. On the other hand, a passion for righteousness needs to be allied to a gentle nature if insensitive, callous bigotry is not to be the result.

The world is full of groups who claim to be hungering and thirsting for righteousness. Some of these groups are building hospitals; others are filling hospital beds with the human carnage they create. Some are building schools, while others are claiming that most schooling is building into pupils an acceptance of existing unrighteousness. Some are crusading to liberate us sexually, while others are branding this liberation as licence to be stamped out.

So how do we know what righteousness really is? The various ideas of righteousness and justice that are championed throughout our world are often mutually contradictory.

To Jesus— and indeed to most of his hearers who were schooled in Hebrew traditions—righteousness was not a matter of opinion or politics. It had to do with the very nature of Almighty God. It was not so much that the Hebrews first had an idea of righteousness and then recognized that this could be applied to their God as a description. Rather it was that their notions of righteousness came from their knowledge of God. God is righteousness, and therefore all that is not righteous is not of God. God in his nature is the very source of righteousness. One modern translation of this Beatitude is: "Blessed are those who hunger and thirst to do which God requires." It is a pretty accurate way of bringing home the meaning. Righteousness is never defined in the Old Testament, it is taken for granted as—God's requirements.

However there are plenty of instances that are branded as righteous (or otherwise) in the Old Testament and from these we can draw general principles.

Amos was a countryman from near Bethlehem in the kingdom of Judah, which was one of the two kingdoms into which the Jewish people had divided themselves after the reign of Solomon. While visiting the northern kingdom of Israel he became appalled at what he saw. There was corruption, gross sexual immorality, and terrible exploitation of the poor. And yet in the middle of all this he found that worship was well attended. This was not considered to be contradiction. In some religions today, including perhaps nominal, established Christianity, it still is not so considered. Many feel that the quest for spiritual enlightenment has nothing to do with one's attitude to one's neighbor.

Not so Amos. He thundered against what he saw until he was forcibly silenced. No amount of religious observances could make up for the fact that God wanted justice to "roll down like waters, and righteousness like an everflowing stream" (Amos 5:24). Amos was specific in mentioning such matters as traders giving false measure, people being used as payments of debts in a sort of slavery-cum-hostage basis; people enjoying affluence while being surrounded by dire poverty among other sections of the community; prostitution—which may or may not have religious significance; and those in positions of power taking bribes.

All this was "unrighteous." It was against the will and requirements of God. Old Testament religion did not, therefore, divorce the spiritual from the social and political. Other prophets, such as Isaiah, Micah, and Hosea were equally clear on this matter. The spiritual rebellion of God's ancient people was evidenced in their social disorder. It was not enough to go through the motions of worship; there had to be a way of life that was also an act of worship.

Much earlier in Hebrew history Moses returned to the camp of the traveling nation after prolonged absence on the mysterious slopes of Mount Sinai. He brought with him ten commandments which were to be observed by those who counted themselves as members of God's special people. The first group of these commandments dealt with a man's relationship to God, but most of the commandments concerned men's relationships with one another. There had to be respect for authority in the home because this was the basic unit of society and a breakdown at that point could threaten the survival of a tribe or nation. The taking of life was forbidden. So also was adultery, stealing, and false witness concerning other people. Finally there came a commandment that moved from acts into attitudes. God condemned covetousness.

From all this it can be seen that the commandments are not about one's private goodness but about orderly communal living. The sort of society God required valued people in themselves. It was comprised of families which were disciplined, based on marriages that were recognized and externally protected by custom. It recognized ownership, property, truth, and the importance of fair dealings between its members. This sort of society also would acknowledge the existence and supremacy of God; would attempt no paring-down of his distinctive greatness and would allow nothing and no one to rival his supreme position in the affection and loyalty of individuals and society. The ten commandments are a unit. The commandments affecting the social are grounded on those affecting the spiritual. In fact the spiritual and social are one and the same.

James recognized this oneness in his New Testament epistle. In a section where he discusses people's inability to control the tongue, he says: "With it we bless the Lord and Father, and with it we curse men, who are made in the likeness of God. . . . This ought not to be so" (James 3:9-10). Clearly James inherited the Old Testament understanding that life does not have a religious compartment and a secular one. What is wrong among men is wrong before God. It is important to see that the leading figure in the Jerusalem Christian church was fully in line with the Old Testament prophets on these matters because a superficial reading of the New Testament could lead to the false view that righteousness is a religious and spiritual business entirely to do with our relationship to God (or lack of it).

Of course it is most certainly not *right* that we are wrong with God! This is the most basic unrighteousness of all. And the New Testament writers were agreed that nothing we could do of ourselves could put right our basic wrongness with God. The good news they had for their readers was that Jesus had, in his death, suffered the consequences of our sin. He died as "the just for the unjust," and because of this we could pass muster with the heavenly Father because our wrongs were "covered" by Christ's overwhelming righteousness.

But although this is the heart of the New Testament teaching on righteousness it is by no means the whole of it. And if we try to understand Christ's Beatitude entirely in terms of this notion of needing

71

the cover of Christ's righteousness, then we are likely to make two mistakes.

The first is to limit unrighteousness to personal and private sins. The second is to think that after becoming Christians there is nothing we can do about the righteousness business because Jesus has done it all. What in fact Jesus has done is to deal with the basic unrighteousness of men being lost in their sins and cut off from God their Creator-Father. Through his death and resurrection forgiveness can be offered to all of us. But this does not mean that we are meant to continue to accept unrighteousness all around us. Jesus, through his life, death, and resurrection has not dealt with social unrighteousness. That task he has left to those who follow him. To ignore social unrighteousness is to continue in sin.

To return to the prophets and, in this case, Isaiah. One of his phrases which Christian preachers are fond of quoting is as follows:

> Come now, let us reason together, says the Lord: though your sins are like scarlet, they shall be as white as snow. (Isa. 1:18)

The picture is moving and comforting. The forgiving Father can utterly wipe out our spoiled record from before his eyes and treat us as if we are perfect. Unfortunately Christian preachers are apt to give the impression that the sins Isaiah is talking about are to do with our unbelief, our selfishness, our lack of prayer, our imperfect thoughts about sex, and so on.

One has only to look at the words in Isaiah which precede this favorite text:

> Learn to do good;
> seek justice,
>     correct oppression;
> defend the fatherless,
>     plead for the widow.
>     (Isa. 1:17)

The matter is not a case of either/or. We must see that righteousness is a massive thing affecting both our private relationship with God and our public dealing with men. God is grieved by our lack of prayer, but he is equally grieved by the fact that we may be totally uninterested in and detached from social injustices about us. Again there are echoes of the prophet's teaching in James's epistle. Long before arguments and experiments about public welfare, James wrote: "Religion that is pure and undefiled before God and the Father is this: to visit orphans and widows in their affliction, and to keep oneself unstained from the world" (James 1:27).

And James grew up with Jesus sharing the same early training in the Hebrew scriptures. And Jesus said: *"Blessed are those who hunger and thirst for righteousness, for they shall be satisfied."* So we are back to our starting point.

I believe the detour into both Old and New Testaments has been important because we must see Christ's words about righteousness in the light of this total spiritual and social thinking. I do not believe it makes sense to say that these words of

73

Jesus are only to do with acceptance by God. Jesus did not teach anything contrary to Paul's insight that we can be forgiven exactly as we are merely for the asking. It does not therefore make sense that we have to hunger and thirst for the covering righteousness which God freely offers us. Further, this interpretation does not square with the words a few verses later when Jesus speaks of being "persecuted for righteousness' sake" and reminds his listeners that "so men persecuted the prophets who were before you."

Let me put the point starkly. The followers of Jesus are meant to be inwardly pained by unrighteousness in any form. They are meant to be people who want to put things right. They have no mandate from their master to pick out the need for reconciliation with God and only act in this area.

Unfortunately our record shows that we have far too easily settled for a spiritual idea of unrighteousness and give the appearance of uninterest in the very areas that taxed Amos, Isaiah, Micah, Hosea— Old Testament heroes that we read about faithfully and yet somehow avoid relating to our own times. I have been told that one of the reasons why many thoughtful present-day Jews discount Jesus as Messiah is that they see so little concern for social righteousness among his followers.

Having said this, however, one has to face the fact that the earliest Christians spoken about in the Acts of the Apostles do not seem to have been concerned about righteousness in the way that I have been mentioning. They seem rather to have been evangelizing and dealing with the spiritual dimension almost to the exclusion of anything else.

Is this true? Does it cast a new light on what Jesus meant? Should we not follow their examples?

First of all, I think the point must be accepted. Paul, Barnabas, Luke, Peter, and the others were primarily evangelists. We must not ignore, however, the place of healing in their ministry. They were far more than message bearers.

Secondly, however, I would argue against their example being taken as a model for the present day. It is not so much that they dismissed the importance of social action. Rather it was a simple matter of *possibilities*. Amos and his fellow prophets lived in a situation where the powers-that-be acknowledged (in theory at least) the place of a "word of God." Jewish people were running Jewish states in Israel and Judah, and in both communities lip service at least was paid to the importance of the God of Moses and Abraham.

This was not the situation in the world of the New Testament. The Romans were governing in Judea and in Asia Minor and Europe. Wherever Paul and his fellow apostles traveled they were confronted with a situation where their word from God had no standing with either government or the governed. They could hardly point out the implications of their religion where there was no one who professed the religion in the first place. They had to start at square one by introducing their hearers to the God who is the source of all righteousness. They were in a nonbelief situation, not a nominal-belief situation. To go back to the pattern of the Sermon on the Mount, they were calling another generation of hearers to go up, sit at the Master's feet, and discover his teaching.

Nevertheless we can see in the correspondence of those early Christians (the epistles) a clear attempt to establish the righteous way of life of a new people of God. This "new Israel" observed more than a set of teachings. It pursued a way of life that marked it out in sharp relief from the surrounding peoples. Thus we find Peter telling his readers to "live such good lives among the pagans that, though they accuse you of doing wrong, they may see your good deeds and glorify God on the day he visits us" (I Pet. 2:12 NEV). In this particular passage Peter explicitly urges good citizenship and respect for rulers upon his readers. And yet he is aware that this model behavior will not necessarily bring them wholesale approval. They may well be wrongfully accused and punished. When he contemplates this possibility he holds up the example of Jesus. To suffer for doing right is "commendable before God" (I Pet. 2:20), indeed it is "blessed" (I Pet. 3:14) (and here Peter uses precisely the same word as did Jesus in the Beatitude).

The theme of Christians being strangers within their own countries who live as distinct communities and who are "eager to do what is good" (I Pet. 3:13 TEV) is the dominant one in Peter's first epistle. It is spelled out at length in the second and third chapters. They are not to attack the status quo of their surrounding communities so much as to develop a better and more righteous community within. Constantly Peter shows that he is aware that this will bring a backlash from surrounding society and as Christ did not resist his own crucifiers so Christians must be prepared to suffer unjustly for doing right and being good.

Peter's first epistle was addressed to "God's elect, strangers in the world, scattered throughout Pontus, Galatia, Cappadocia, Asia and Bithynia" (I Pet. 1:1). James's epistle is addressed to "the twelve tribes scattered among the nations" (James 1:1). Almost certainly James was speaking symbolically about Christians as representatives of a new Israel who were living throughout the known world in scattered communities exactly as representatives of the old Israel were then living. As with Peter's epistle there is a great deal of talk about the way his readers should be living. It must be remembered that this letter was not a message to the world but some practical advice to Christian communities. It is all the more significant therefore that we find a passage like this:

> Now listen, you rich people, weep and wail because of the misery that is coming to you. Your wealth has rotted, and moths have eaten your clothes. Your gold and silver are corroded. Their corrosion will testify against you and eat your flesh like fire. You have hoarded wealth in the last days. Look! The wages you failed to pay the workmen who mowed your fields are crying out against you. The cries of the harvesters have reached the ears of

the Lord All-powerful. You have lived on earth in luxury and self-indulgence. You have fattened yourselves in the day of slaughter. You have condemned and murdered innocent men, who were not opposing you. (James 5:1-6 NEV)

The whole passage is full of echoes of the Old Testament, from God hearing the cry of the oppressed Israelites in Egypt, to Amos thundering at the opulent callousness of people in Judah. The startling thing is that these words needed to be said *within* Christian communities so early after the time of Christ's earthly days. But then mammon is a subtle rival to God himself. For us today, especially those of us living in the wealthy Western democracies, the message is so clear we can hardly bear it.

*It is not righteous that there should be great disparities in personal wealth.* I have heard Christians try to wriggle out of this, but they will find little help from their Bibles. Often we argue that wealth is *spiritually dangerous* and that it is all too easy to be rich in material goods and desperately poor toward God. Of course Jesus certainly taught this. But we cannot leave it there. Our answer is usually to say, "Don't worry, I'm aware of the danger and I will not let my riches keep me from worshiping God." But it is not so easy to leave it at this point.

In James's condemnation of wealth he points out that the rich people he is attacking have gained their wealth unjustly. "The wages you failed to pay the workmen . . . are crying out against you." Wealth in this case had been amassed through exploitation.

The Old Testament prophets said the same thing. In a simple rural community a man could only be wealthy at someone else's expense. But James goes further. There has not only been exploitation, there has been violence and murder in the pursuit of amassing wealth. The link therefore is drawn between wealth exploitation and violence. It is true that James seems to be referring to some specific cases rather than theorizing in general, but the Hebrew ways of thinking in concrete terms may well mean that the passage is meant as a general observation.

We tend to shrug off the constant evidence that Jesus was opposed to the retention of wealth, but we must stop doing this and try to look at those passages with fresh eyes. In the Sermon on the Mount Jesus said: "Do not lay up for yourselves treasures on earth. . . . For where your treasure is, there will your heart be also" (Matt. 6:19-20). In Luke's account of the Beatitudes he records that Jesus had actually said "Blessed are you poor" (Luke 6:20). When Matthew was called to follow Jesus he was clearly given a choice between his moneymaking and his Master. Luke notes "he left everything, and rose and followed him" (Luke 5:28). Then there is the famous phrase "You cannot serve God and mammon" (Matt. 6:24). The kingdom of heaven was worth selling everything one had to possess (Matt. 14:44), and the rich young ruler was advised to sell everything he had and to give it to the poor—a challenge he could not face as he walked sadly away. This incident gave rise to the Lord's famous phrase: "It is easier for a camel to go through the eye of a needle than for a rich man to enter the kingdom of God" (Mark 10:25).

And so one can go on heaping up the evidence of Christ's warnings about wealth and his disapproval of its retention. In the encounter with the crooked tax collector Zacchaeus, Jesus reserved his statement about salvation coming to the extortioner's house until he heard Zacchaeus say: "Behold, Lord, the half of my goods I give to the poor; and if I have defrauded any one of anything, I restore it fourfold" (Luke 19:8).

The most telling part of his teaching was, in fact, his own station in life. When God chose to come as a man upon the earth, *he came as a poor man.* As in the case of his baptism, I believe this was to "fulfill all righteousness" (Matt. 3:15).

What does this mean for us today? At the very least it means that today's disciple must look at the present goal of ever increasing affluence and prosperity with a highly critical eye. Further, he is only able to do this if he or she is pursuing a personal life-style that is not materialistic and affluent. We need to take the motif in James's epistle with its syndrome of wealth, exploitation, and violence, and see if it is taking place behind all the plastic packaging that gift wraps our ready acceptance of much more than— *enough.* Today as we see higher prices being charged for raw materials and food-stuffs as the underdeveloped countries start holding out for more, we need to ask not, Why are things so expensive now? so much as, Why were things so cheap then?

We need to be asking whether our communities are paying realistic prices for what they expect to receive and use. It is no longer true that we live in simple communities where a man gets wealthy at his immediate neighbor's expense. The community is now complex and worldwide—a Global Village is what it has been called. Instead of one man dealing with another and possibly exploiting him, we now have nations and blocks of nations dealing with other nations and blocks of nations—and possibly exploiting. The world is divided into rich nations and poor nations and somehow, in spite of all the fine talk, it seems the disparity increases rather than otherwise. We who hunger and thirst for righteousness cannot be at ease about this. It should cause us to mourn. But mourning that is confined to words and conference resolutions is of little value. What is needed is action and this is where we feel so helpless. We put the world to rights in our discussion groups and then walk out into a real world that is unchanged, and this leads to a quiet background conviction that there is nothing we can do.

I believe we can do something. We can say, as did Joshua of old in a crisis situation: "as for me and my house, we will serve the Lord" (Josh. 24:15). We can work to set up within our Christian congregations, righteous communities which are models for the world at large. We can prove that simpler lives can be happier lives. We can live more modestly, use fewer commodities, and share more among ourselves. Already Christians are trying this whether it be in

81

the much publicized Holy Redeemer Church of Houston, Texas, or the Jesus Liberation Front of Hemel Hempstead in England. We have seen that James and Peter wrote epistles to the scattered Christian communities of their day urging a style of living that would make them clearly identified as righteous—a style that called for fearing God, honoring the emperor, loving the brotherhood, and honoring all men (I Pet. 2:17). They believed it was "God's will *that by doing right*" they "should put to silence the ignorance of foolish men" (I Pet. 2:15).

This is where we must begin. We must take Christ out of our minds and into our money-matters; out of our discussions and into our decisions; out of our creeds and into our conduct; and out of our private lives and into our communities. It is only when surrounding society can see a recognizable group of Christian communities that we will have the right to make recommendations to them and pass resolutions in our conferences. This does not mean waiting until we are perfect in these matters; we shall never be. But others must be able to acknowledge that we are attempting to set our own houses in order.

Of course righteousness covers far more than our use or abuse of wealth, but I have felt it right to emphasize this area because I believe we are all running away from what the Bible clearly implies at this point. Further I believe this is the key area in our times. We are living at one of those turning points in world history, and so much is hinging on wealth and what money can buy for individuals and for nations.

The Western world is beginning to wake up to some of the unhappy implications of affluence, but it has not yet got the will or motivation to change direction. The official religion of Europe and America is not Christianity but materialism, and we have not yet clearly identified our false idol. We have all been schooled to think we have the right to possess more than enough. We need a great deal of de-schooling, but Christians have a thrilling opportunity to give a lead.

Again, you cannot separate wealth and power. The degree of wealth we possess determines how much freedom of choice and opportunity we have, what sort of health we will enjoy, what sort of education is possible for our children, whether we eat or whether we starve. If it is true that in today's world we can only have more than enough at the expense of others having less than enough then it is with the matter of wealth that we must begin. And we must begin with ourselves or we are hypocritical humbugs.

But Jesus foresaw that his followers would be persecuted for the sake of righteousness. There may not be the pleasure of success for those of us who are anxious to do right. There may well be frustrations. There will be, however, the profound satisfaction of knowing that we are doing God's will, and that is *real* happiness!

# CHAPTER 7
## *THE GODLY INFECTION*

The biggest reality for the Christian is that he is a forgiven person. It was this realization that drove Paul of Tarsus to forget what lay behind and to press ever onward in the service of his Lord.

Jesus was very clear in his teaching, however, that forgiveness was not merely some initial God-to-man transaction that started off one's personal Christianity, but rather a mark of the way of life of his new people. In his pattern prayer he taught us to ask for forgiveness only if we were prepared to offer it to others. In the Beatitudes we read "Blessed are the merciful for they shall obtain mercy," and one of Christ's most penetrating parables is about the relationship of our own forgiveness to that mercy we extend toward our fellows.

He told of a king (Matt. 18:23-35) who found that one of his servants owed him a huge sum of money. The figure Jesus used in his story—ten thousand talents—was an unattainable sum to almost any man, let alone a servant. The poor servant pleaded for time to raise and repay the money. The alternative was the selling of everything he had including himself, wife and children, into slavery. The servant's request was ridiculous, but the king had compassion and so he "released him and forgave him the debt."

But the story did not end at this point. We read:

> That same servant, as he went out, came upon one of his fellow servants who owed him a hundred denarii [a very small sum]; and seizing him by the throat he said, "Pay me what you owe." So his fellow servant fell down and besought him, "Have patience with me, and I will pay you." He refused and went and put him in prison till he should pay the debt. (Matt. 18:28-30)

The contrast between the size of the debts and the attitudes of the two creditors is stark and clear. Jesus went on to relate the awesome punishment that the king eventually meted out to the unforgiving servant. His conclusion was: "So also my heavenly Father will do to every one of you, if you do not forgive your brother from your heart" (Matt. 18:35).

There is one matter that can escape notice in this familiar story. This is that the unforgiving servant was perfectly within his rights to do what he did. The customs and laws of his time allowed him to insist on repayments and to realize his assets in terms of enslaving those who were in his debt. Jesus never denied that the unforgiving servant had rights in his favor. The point was that for his part the servant had huge debts to his king and that the king had not insisted on *his* rights. So why should the unforgiving servant operate by *rights* when his freedom had been secured through his king operating by *mercy*?

The New Testament often contrasts mercy with

justice. To be merciful is not to insist on rights but to recognize *needs*. The point of the parable is obvious. We are hopelessly in debt to a holy and righteous God. If he is to operate in terms of *rights* we are doomed. As the psalmist puts it:

> If thou, O Lord, shouldst mark iniquities
> Lord, who could stand? (Ps. 130:3)

But the psalmist does not end there. "There is forgiveness with thee . . ." he continues. Every single Christian is a forgiven person. He is a member of the heavenly Father's new eternal family because God has been merciful toward him and set aside his rights. This is the way the Father of the family works—it must be our way also.

So Jesus urged his first followers to find the happiness of foregoing their rights, recognizing others' needs, making allowances, and being merciful. He pointed out that mercy would bring mercy in return.

It is worth remembering Peter's question which gave rise to the Lord's parable. "Lord," he asked, "How often shall my brother sin against me, and I forgive him? As many as seven times?" (Matt. 18:21). The parable was Christ's way of replying.

How then are we to look at the uncomfortable fact that our Christian churches are often full of differences of opinion, petty contentions, rivalries and squabbles? Like many preachers I have often reacted to this and made sweeping statements about love in the New Testament church; as if our churches since then had *discovered* squabbling! The fact is that the New Testament epistles were nearly all written to try to settle squabbles!

I have come to see that squabbles can often in fact be signs of life and fellow-feeling, rather than the opposite. When I travel by train, bus, or plane the chances are that I shall find myself one of a number of passengers all sitting in orderly rows waiting for the journey to finish. It is highly unlikely that we shall find ourselves squabbling with one another. At the same time it is highly unlikely that such a group should be called a fellowship or a family. We are all keeping ourselves to ourselves and living in our own separate worlds. To call this a peaceful fellowship would show a total misunderstanding of the meaning of peace and the meaning of fellowship. The last thing we want is for our churches to resemble such orderly non-communities!

The moment people start being themselves and trying to relate to one another we have a situation where friction is not only possible but highly likely. As a father of three I know what I am talking about! While I often wish family mealtimes were more restful I should be very worried if they resembled a meal served in a restaurant full of strangers! The mistake that conscientious Christians often make is to lament "divisions in the church" when they should be seeing these disruptions as signs of life—yes, and of caring. We need to be clear in our minds about the distinctive nature of unity among Christians. It is not blissful regimentation and uniformity. It is rather the co-ordination under a gracious God of different people, different gifts, and even different points of view. Such co-ordination under a gracious God of different people, different gifts, and even different points of view. Such co-ordination is so delicate that there will rarely be times when there are not cracks in the wholeness at some point and between some people. Indeed the more convinced and dedicated each Christian is, the more chances there are of tension because what people are arguing about is their respective ideas about *God's* will rather than their own.

The ideal Christian fellowship, this side of heaven, will not, therefore be placid—but it would be merciful. The key to such a fellowship holding together and not shattering into a thousand pieces is the realization on the part of all members of their personal forgiven-ness. This is the great motivation for being forgiving. Just as "we love because he first loved us" so we forgive because he first forgave us, and we exercise mercy because we continually need to receive mercy. The mark of Christian friendship is not the absence of arguments but the facility for forgiveness. Reconciliation is always going on.

Here again we see that the Beatitudes are all of a piece. Proud people cannot cope with either the exercise or receipt of mercy, but the person who recognizes his poverty of spirit can readily do so.

This is an area where we are prone to retreat into fantasy. We either lament our lack of spirituality because a fellowship is divided, or we put on blinkers and try to pretend that we don't have differences, tensions, and latent rifts. This latter course can be disastrous. I can think of a group of Christians engaged in a team activity who refused to acknowledge the differences of opinion that were present on the team. They tried to pretend the differences were not there, but of course they remained and became more serious. Finally there were alignments within the team and a division into two clear factions. Eventually the larger faction moved swiftly to expel the smaller faction. There was, at the time of the expulsion, much talk on both sides about *rights*. There was very little talk, or evidence, of mercy. I have seen the pattern recur in churches and committees on several occasions.

The Beatitude on mercy, however, means more than the practice of forgiveness. It is always important to see in the Sermon on the Mount that Jesus is speaking as someone in the same tradition as the prophets of the Old Testament. He is, of course, far more than a prophet, but yet he is self-consciously in line with them. God had spoken in earlier days through the prophets (see the opening of the Epistle to the Hebrews); now he was speaking by a son.

This means that it is always helpful to look for Old Testament echoes in the Beatitudes. When we come to the Lord's use of "mercy" it helps to see what this word meant in the old Hebrew scriptures. The Hebrew word for mercy was *chesedh*. It is a word that certainly covers the sense of forgiveness. But it goes further. It has the sense of *out-going kindness*. A key insight into its meaning is to be found in Hosea's words: "I desire steadfast love [*chesedh*] and not sacrifice" (Hos. 6:6). As in the case of Amos, the prophet Hosea was contrasting outward religious observances unfavorably with compassionate kindness. On two occasions Jesus quoted these words of Hosea. Those occasions are worth examining. We shall take the second occasion first.

> At that time Jesus went through the grainfields on the sabbath; his disciples were hungry, and they began to pluck heads of grain and to eat. But when the Pharisees saw it, they said to him, "Look, your disciples are doing what is not lawful to do on the sabbath." He said to them, "Have you not read what David did, when he was hungry, and those who were with him: how he entered the house of God and ate the bread of the Presence, which it was not lawful for him to eat nor for those who were with him, but only for the priests? Or have you not read in the law how on the sabbath the priests in the temple profane the sabbath, and are guiltless? I tell you, something greater than the temple is here. And if you had known what this means, *"I desire mercy, and not sacrifice,"* you would not have condemned the guiltless. (Matt. 12:1-7; my italics.)

This passage relates a situation that became all too common during Christ's ministry. Religious groups were looking for technical religious faults in what Jesus and his followers were doing. On this occasion it was the casual plucking of some grain (which was permissible in normal circumstances and therefore stealing is not being alleged). The fault was that this was work on the sabbath.

The reply of Jesus was threefold. The first point was to show that the great King David had technically broken the religious law when he and his men were hungry, and as King David was the great folk hero of the Jews this point was a strong one. The second point was a tantalizing hint, that he, Jesus, was bringing about "something greater than the temple." The third point was that observances of laws were not more important than the exercise of outgoing kindness. It was at this point that Jesus rebuked his critics for not seeing the meaning of Hosea's words.

Let us look at the other instance when Jesus recalled Hosea's phrase.

> As Jesus passed on from there, he saw a man called Matthew sitting at the tax office; and he said to him, "Follow me." And he rose and followed him.
>
> And as he sat at table in the house, behold, many tax collectors and sinners came and sat down with Jesus and his disciples. And when the Pharisees saw this, they said to his disciples, "Why does your teacher eat with tax collectors and sinners?" But when he heard it, he said, "Those who are well have no need of a physician, but those who are sick. Go and learn what this means, '*I desire mercy, and not sacrifice.*' For I come not to call the righteous, but sinners." (Matt. 9:9-13; my italics.)

Matthew the tax collector would have been a despised person. The tax collector of those times was a collaborationist with the occupying power and operated by sets of rules that he made up to suit himself and his own pocket. For Jesus to even talk to such a person was a public scandal to the pious Jew. To attend a meal in such a man's house was, of course, infinitely more disgraceful. Yet Jesus had no qualms on the matter. When criticized he spoke of the doctor attending to the sick rather than the healthy—and reminded his critics of Hosea's words.

Clearly Jesus disapproved of extortion, which was Matthew's stock-in-trade. That did not prevent him showing outgoing kindness toward the offender. Further he took the initiative in the transaction. Matthew was not, as far as we can see, a man becoming disgusted with himself and contemplating quitting his crooked ways. Jesus simply went up to him in an accepting spirit and called him to follow. The impact was profound and immediate.

If the Pharisees had laid down the rules for Jesus he would never have been able to approach Matthew. Rather he would have had to shelter behind a framework of religious scruples and principles. Mercy therefore, as we see it in Jesus, was a liberating attitude that did not deny the importance of the values locked away in the rules of the Pharisees, but saw beyond them to the God who not only exposes our sins but offers forgiveness.

Mercy, as Jesus exhibited it, was not the reward for those who passed some test of approval. It was a gift that was always freely an offer. Often it was spurned. True religion, as he practiced it, was not a personal restriction to codes and practices. It was a demonstration of God's outgoing, initiative-taking, forgiving kindness. This, then, is the pattern for the Christian.

It is important for us to see what this means. It does not mean that doctrine is unimportant and that all that matters is a Christlike spirit. For one thing, the statement that "all that matters is a Christlike spirit" is itself a doctrinal statement! If we believe it we are committed to a doctrine. For another thing, to talk of following the example of Christ's way of life and way of dealing with people is assuming we can trust the picture we have of him in the New Testament—and that is very much to do with doctrinal positions. So it is right to be engaged in the defense of Christian doctrines and principles. If we are not so concerned then the very foundations of our faith could be undermined.

But in daily life the action is where the mercy is! Those of us who are Christ's followers should be known principally for this quality of *chesedh*: mercy, outgoing kindness. Only when we are studied more closely should it become clear that this kindness goes hand in hand with basic beliefs to which we are firmly committed. And when we open up in evangelism to share and to persuade others about our beliefs our listeners should already be clear about one thing—we are the people whose way of life is one of kindness and mercy.

And that kindness and mercy is not one that respects other people's rules either. Let me give a stark example of this. In the years 1966–70 we saw the tragic case of the Nigerian civil war after the breakaway state of Biafra. In passing let it be noted that the victorious Nigerian forces were led by men who gave the world an unparalleled example of mercy and reconciliation when the war was ended. Nevertheless during that war the international Christian community was posed with an agonizing dilemma. In Biafra as the Nigerian forces pressed their attacks, there were starving children. Indeed the Biafran leaders made much political capital out of the matter. Of course many concerned Christians favored the Biafran side in the war. But many others who either refused to take sides or, like myself were opposed to the creation of Biafra, still felt that starving children had to be fed whether it was in the military interests of Nigeria or not. The Nigerians felt—with good cause—that any aid was succoring a doomed rebellion and thereby prolonging a war which was in everyone's interests to stop. It was also clear that aid could be misappropriated and in one way or another benefit the rebel armies.

If the international Christian community had played to the rules and thought in cold objective terms about rights and wrongs they would have held back and done little or nothing. As it was they went in, running the blockade, breaking the rules, ignoring the advice of diplomats. They flew in aid to those children. Mercy had to come first, with the rights and wrongs to be discussed later. It was misunderstood and much aid went to the wrong people, but *it was the only thing for Christians to do*. John wrote, "if anyone has the world's goods and sees his brother in need, yet closes his heart against him, how does God's love abide in him?" (I John 3:17).

94

## THE GODLY INFECTION

In our personal dealings with one another I think we Christians must have the same order of priorities. It will make us vulnerable and open to be either misunderstood or manipulated. It will not automatically bring us a response of love or respect, for the love of Christ was met with a sentence of death. Yet when the full truth is known, to inject mercy in a community is to generate mercy within that same community—of this I am sure.

Unfortunately like so many other Christians I have learned the deeply "spiritual sounding" arguments to employ against doing some things that are merciful, kind, and outgoing. Like so many Christians I am good at discussing doctrinal issues, taking part in conferences, writing articles and books, and just about anything that keeps me from going out to exhibit the mercy and love of God both in material ways and in testimony and preaching. Like, perhaps, the priest and the levite I have learned the respectable religious reasons for hurrying on past the huddled body by the roadside. But my Lord commended the Samaritan who stopped and helped the man in need.

Of course the needs for love and mercy in our world are manifold and overwhelming. Our daily newspapers and our television screens make us observers of a world of suffering much of which seems totally beyond the reach of ourselves and our resources. It seems that we are given a cruel choice. Either we let the news come through and hurt us or we harden our hearts and learn to accept the fact that we are unable to help. But this choice, I believe, is a false one. The response we must make is to start where we are and do what we can. When Jesus told his followers that by doing a kindness to anyone they had done it to him personally, I believe he gave us a formula that can be taken in other ways. The way of helping the person out of reach is to help the person within reach. Mercy is a godly infection. It spreads. Mercy has a built-in multiplication factor. To inject kindness is to create ripples that will spread outward. And the center for each set of ripples must be the Christian congregation.

From a group of people giving and receiving mercy and kindness the infection can spread into all the areas of life to which the congregation members belong—their homes, their neighborhoods, their places of work, their schools, and so on. This, I am sure, is the divine pattern.

When I wrote my first book, *The Gagging of God,* I rather gave the impression of the local church being the cold, calculating teaching and training center from which Christians went out into the world as clued-up communicators. I don't think I gave nearly enough place to the importance of our churches being schools where we learn to practice the godly infection of mercy and kindness. Maybe that was because I had seen very little evidence that churches could ever be like that. But they can be.

And they must be. Anything less cannot be the Body of Christ.

# CHAPTER 8
## *THE PURE AND THE PRUDISH*

It was soon after eight in the morning one Sunday during my first year of life as a curate in an East London Anglican Church. It was my lot at the early morning service of Holy Communion to be reading the epistle, and I had been foolish enough to think I could pick up my prayer book and read it adequately without preparation. Pride—as the saying goes—comes before a fall!

On this occasion the epistle contained the phrase "not in the lusts of concupiscence," and fractionally after I began to read the passage aloud my eye roved ahead and spotted the phrase—and particularly *that word!* Somehow I had a chill premonition that I was going to have difficulty with *concupiscence!* After all, it was hardly a word that popped up, like an old friend, in everyday speech.

Sure enough: when I came to the phrase I made a magnificent hash of it. "Not in the lusts of cuconpisense . . . er concensucupe . . . er cucumbensense . . . er . . ."

Finally I was wise enough to abandon this unequal struggle and I moved on to the easier words that followed. Perhaps it was significant that the congregation was made to chuckle over the "lusts of concupiscence"!

I tell this story not only to introduce the subject of this chapter but also because all through the writing of this book I have been looking ahead with apprehension to the task of writing about purity just as I approached that tongue-twisting word with a sense of awe. I can see two reasons for my apprehension. The first is that, like so many of us, I am loath to appear prudish. Perhaps it is one of the greatest achievements of the opponents of chastity that they have managed to make its defenders reluctant to declare their position with vigor. We have a curious and subtle situation emerging where the upholders of sexual self-control are made to appear heartless. The truth is that nothing is more heartless than casual sex.

What is happening in the debate about sexual self-control is that those who are opposed to chastity have said black equals white so often and so loudly that everyone is beginning to believe it. I have heard Christians accused of being obsessed with sex because they felt obliged to protest about such matters as pornography in the movies, theater, and the paperback rack. Since when has disapproval meant the same thing as obsession? There are no strip-tease shows in our churches. There is no pornography in our church periodicals and Christian publications. And yet some of those who support the commercialization of sex are accusing Christians of being obsessed.

We must ask which is the greater evidence of obsession—theaters that show nothing other than sex films or those groups of people who *occasionally* stand outside and protest?

The truth is that we Christians are obsessed with a grander concept of human sexuality than one advocated by some squalid paperback—and thank God for that! We believe that human sexuality finds its fulfillment in adventurous, lifelong, for-better-for-worse relationships. A selfish round of experimentations is a poor substitute for a triumphant marriage.

And yet, having said this, one has to admit that Christians have, at times, shown heartless condemnation and even hypocrisy in the area of sexual morality. It is easy to forget that some of the finest poems in the Bible were penned by an adulterer. And King David's legal marriages were far from triumphant. Jesus pointed out that adultery can be committed just as certainly in the mind as it can be in the bed, and recognizing this gives no one grounds for heartless condemnation of others. We can very easily be prudish and many of us are. It is also true that a great deal of cluttered Christian tradition has led to some devout people believing that sex is rather unwholesome. Such a view ignores the simple fact that sex was God's idea in the first place.

No, we Christians have been mistaken about sex; dishonest and unrealistic about our own failings and far too little sympathetic toward those who have fallen short of the best. But to admit all these failings is a very different thing from abandoning the grander concept of a lifelong relationship. Those who fail to see or to seek the grander concept need compassion and to be pitied but it helps no one for them to be accommodated.

This leads me to the second reason for being reluctant to write on purity. I am only too aware of my own imperfections in this department of life. However New Testament morality is more to do with *goals* than achievements. As Paul was discussing the goal of "gaining Christ" on one occasion he summed up his position in the following words: "Not that I have already obtained this or am already perfect; but I press on to make it my own . . . press on towards the goal" (Phil. 3:12-14). This is the healthy consciousness of any Christian with regard to moral and spiritual matters. This does not mean an attitude of defeatism or self-incrimination. It means rather a constant awareness that if our moral and spiritual achievements were to be the means of our acceptance by God, we would never make the grade. Indeed it is all tucked away in the opening Beatitude—"Blessed are the poor in spirit, for theirs is the kingdom of heaven." Salvation is the Father's free offer for us all. Nevertheless, out of gratitude and a desire to bear witness to the standards of our Father, it is right to have goals for our behavior. So forgetting the failures that may have strewn our path in the past we press on.

However the purity that Jesus referred to in the Beatitudes was much more than a sexual purity. It was a purity *of the heart*—something that affected the whole of life. In this sense we again have a helpful insight from seeing Christ's words against an Old Testament background. The Greek version of the Old Testament uses this same word for purity *(katharos)* in two different ways. The main use is to describe *ritual* purity such as the purity of a priest. Now this purity was purely *external*. A priest merely had to belong to the right family and to be free from certain physical defects and he was considered pure for his ceremonial tasks. His morals, his thought-life, and his habits had nothing to do with the purity that was required. This ritual purity was the sort of purity that would come to the minds of a Hebrew crowd listening to Jesus. But Jesus talked to them about being pure *in heart*. This had to do with *internal* matters which was a very different kettle of fish. It was much more demanding.

But even there, the call of Christ for inner purity was not without its Old Testament echoes either. In Psalm 24 we read:

> Who shall ascend the hill of the Lord?
>   And who shall stand in his holy place?
> He who has clean hands and a pure heart,
>   who does not lift up his soul to what is false,
>   and does not swear deceitfully.
>
> (Vs. 3-4)

The idea of inner purity as something far greater, more demanding, and more pleasing to God is clearly in the Old Testament as well as the more familiar external purity. Jesus merely pointed it up as the purity that is more important.

The contrast between external and internal purity is far more than something of passing historical interest. It strikes deep at the heart of contemporary Christianity. We so easily make for ourselves a religion of outward things—churchgoing, personal disciplines regarding attendance at Holy Communion, daily prayer and Bible reading, attendance at some prayer group, and so on. Of course all of these things are good and valuable in themselves. But they can easily become unrelated to our attitudes to work, money-making, relationships, politics, spending, and so on. What purity of heart is all about is consistent, integrated Christian character.

One of the constant factors in all the Greek Old Testament uses of the word *Katharos,* whether in the outword sense or in the inward sense, is this idea of unblemishedness, unmixed pureness—indeed, in the sense that we talk of *pure gold.* We are meant to be pure Christians not as a contrast to being lecherous Christians but as a contrast to being partial Christians. And this is where it really hits home to us. Some of us may find no temptation whatsoever to be untrue to our wives, or to sleep around before marriage, or even (though I find it hard to believe with present-day pressures) to entertain salacious thoughts; but we can still be dreadfully impure in our business dealings, in the way we play football, or spend our money. This comprehensive purity is what Jesus was talking about, and I find it daunting indeed. In achievement terms, how can we find happiness when facing such an impossible challenge?

The answer takes us back to what I said earlier. Christian morality is a matter of pursuing goals rather than counting up achievements. Every day, because of the forgiveness of God, we can write off our past failures and press on in our attempts to obey God. And the Holy Spirit is given to those who set out to obey. There are only two alternatives to this inner life. One is to enter a world of fantasy and pretend we are perfect or can be. This way leads to disillusion at some time or other. The other way is to wallow in self-criticism and guilt. This way leads to despair.

One thing I have learned over the years is the folly of what one might call a hygienic understanding of inner purity. In this hygienic approach one becomes conscious of the need to *keep out* impurities such as salacious thoughts, anger and so on. In the nature of things it becomes a losing battle and Jesus' parable about the soul being swept clean and therefore ready to be occupied not only by the demon that used to live there but by others also, should act as a warning against this negative understanding of purity.

Purity is more likely to be attained by *crowding out* the impurities rather than by attempts at *keeping out*. This, I think, is what lies behind Paul's helpful words to his Philippian friends:

> Whatever is true, whatever is honorable, whatever is just, whatever is pure, whatever is lovely, whatever is gracious, if there is any excellence, if there is anything worthy of praise, think about these things. (Phil. 4:8)

A mind packed with the things that bear witness to God is the best basis for internal and external purity whether it be with regard to sexual behavior or to one's language when you miss a ten-inch putt!

All this talk of a goal-directed purity touches the contemporary Christian at another point. It may well be that the day of reckoning will show twentieth-century Western Christians as the most goalless, aimless believers in church history. It would be a revealing, perhaps shattering, experience to stop members of the average congregation as they left church one Sunday and ask them What are your goals in life? Many, I am sure, would assure the questioner that their goals were "to serve Christ" or "to be better Christians."

But such answers beg the question. In what ways is Christ asking his followers to serve him in today's world? What makes a Christian *better*? I have mentioned earlier in this book that many Christians today are interested in *power*. But I ask—is this power for its own sake? If not, what is the power for?

Again I suggest we are helped toward answers if we see that the Beatitudes are all of a piece. They speak not only of attitudes but also of actions. Supremely there is the struggle for righteousness in our world and linked with this is the outgoing kindness of those who show mercy and who work for peace and reconciliation in human affairs. We begin where we are. And in the pursuit of these goals where we are, there comes the single-mindedness that makes for purity.

The end product of all this is that we shall see God! "Blessed are the pure in heart, for they shall see God." Many of us are, in fact, trying to take shortcuts to the place where we can see God. This inner ability to see God at work in our world, in nature, in people, in the stringing together of events and situations is not meant to be a goal in itself but rather the by-product of a goal. It comes from the pursuit of those goals that integrate us as Christians, moving us from being partial to being pure. Paul saw this clearly when he challenged his readers in Rome with the words:

> I urge you, brothers, in view of God's mercy, to offer yourselves as living sacrifices, holy and pleasing to God—which is your spiritual worship. Do not conform any longer to the pattern of this world, but be transformed by the renewing of your mind. Then you will be able to test and approve what God's will is—his pleasing and perfect will. (Rom. 12:1-2 NIV)

Paul speaks here of being "able to test and approve what God's will is." It amounts to the same thing as Christ's promise to "see God," for he was referring not to visions but to an inner eye of discernment. The development of this inner eye comes as a by-product of the living sacrifice of our*selves*—our minds, our emotions, our hands, our lips, our ears, our eyes, our feet, in fact everything about us.

To have any goal in life brings a sense of purpose and fulfillment. To have God's goals brings the new happiness of which Jesus spoke, whether those goals are attained or whether they are not.

# CHAPTER 9
## *MAKE PEACE, NOT "LOVE"!*

On a hot, sweltering July day in New York I stopped one of the city's famous yellow cabs, got in, and settled back in the seat as we clattered over the uneven streets toward a destination I have since forgotten.

But I have never forgotten the driver. Each New York cab has the driver's photograph and name on display on a sort of identity card fixed to the dashboard. I could see from the name that the driver was Jewish. We got to talking, and he turned out to be someone actually born in Israel. We were soon discussing the tragic Arab-Israeli confrontation, which was especially relevant as the papers were full of the news of the assassination in Washington of an Israeli diplomat.

He spoke with great feeling. "I pray for peace every night," he said—and I believed him. We compared our various views as to how the crisis might be solved, and as he negotiated the cab through the city, I, a Christian, and he, a Jew, found an affinity that made that ride one of the best memories of my trip to the United States.

As I paid, tipped, and got out I couldn't resist

giving him a greeting I had never used before. *"Shalom,"* I said—hoping it wasn't the wrong thing to do. He half turned to me and said quietly, with great feeling: *"Shalom—shalom!"*

*Shalom* means—*peace.*

Perhaps few words have become more evocative and moving in recent years than this simple word— *peace.* The pacifists have tried to make it their private possession, the communists have made it a form of propaganda, and in some places the associations surrounding the word have made it a suspect concept. Contemporary protest singers have moved audiences to tears singing about peace, and the great movement in the late sixties to get American soldiers out of the Vietnam war was often called a peace movement.

The peace Jesus talked about in the Beatitudes was something very different. He spoke about *shalom,* for that was the only concept that his Hebrew listeners understood. And *shalom* means more than our notion of peace. A perfect example of this is, in fact, the false peace that came from American soldiers withdrawing from Vietnam. That was a negative notion. It was hoped that the reduction of belligerence would bring peace. The truth was otherwise. Vietnam needed more than one lot of soldiers going home. It needed reconciliation and the healing of divisions—but the diplomats didn't think enough in those sorts of terms. They, like the peace campaigners in America, thought of peace by subtraction—but that isn't *shalom.* It isn't the peace that Jesus talked about.

*Shalom* is about peace through *addition*. It doesn't remove the strife—it transforms it through the addition of love, care, and help. There are two main meanings to *shalom*. The first is prosperity and contentment. The second is to do with goodwill and fellowship between men.

We have an English saying about "peace at any price." It is seldom used with approval and rightly so, because peace cannot in fact be bought at any price. Isaiah wrote: "The effect of righteousness will be peace." True peace is always accompanied by righteousness because unrighteous attempts to pacify a situation will only build time bombs for future explosions. Perhaps the seeds of the Second World War were sown in the humiliating terms of peace imposed upon the Germans after the First.

And in social relationships this link is necessary. Peace within a nation cannot be achieved if one section of the community is in a position to exploit another, or if one section of the community is suffering from the effects of unrighteousness. A totalitarian regime which suppresses the aspirations of the people is in no sense peaceful even if the repression is effective in preventing any protest. Sooner or later the time bomb will go off.

Again the management of a company that has no concern for the prosperity, well-being and good relationships of its employees will not be free from industrial unrest. Righteousness is needed among men if there is to be real peace among men. The Bible on several occasions notes the link between righteousness and peace (Ps. 72:3; Ps. 85:10; Hebrews 7:1, 2, and especially James 3:18). It is no coincidence that both words figure prominently in the Beatitudes.

One of Paul's great points in the early chapters of Romans is that our peace with God was not bought at "any price" either. He held that "the wages of sin is death" (Rom. 6:23) but that those wages had been paid in full to Jesus Christ on our behalf. He is therefore "our righteousness" (I Cor. 1:30) according to Paul and being "justified" (i.e. made *righteous*) "by faith, we have *peace* with God through our Lord Jesus Christ" (Rom. 5:1). The only peace that can exist between the believer and his heavenly Father is a righteous peace.

This link between righteousness and real peace is important to see and in the emotional climate that often surrounds the use of the word "peace" the link is often overlooked. Peace at any price is never real peace. Peace is not the same thing as appeasement. Peace can never be achieved while ignoring the claims of justice.

It is worth looking at another often-used phrase—"make love, not war." This is a slogan that has been used, particularly by the young and idealistic, in recent years. It sounds lovely and moving. In fact the phrase when analyzed reveals its built-in shallowness. First of all it speaks about this false idea of peace by subtraction. It speaks of the desirable end of "not war." But, as we have seen, "not war" is a very much lesser thing than the peace Jesus talked about.

Then again the phrase exalts the making of love. And the tongue-in-cheek reference is to the modern usage of that phrase namely, sexual intercourse. Quite apart from the fact that love is far more than sex, and quite apart from the fact that many types of sexual relationship are unrighteous, the slogan would be pretty poor advice to an embattled military commander or to a sincerely intentioned diplomat who cannot get his opposite number to negotiate or to an industrial arbitrator trying to stop a strike!

On the other hand there is a grain of truth in the slogan. If we take it to mean *"wage love not war"* then it is indeed speaking of *shalom. Shalom* requires love, which is another way of saying that *shalom* requires humility, deep concern, meekness, desire for righteousness, outgoing kindness, and mercy—in fact the very qualities and attitudes that Jesus spoke about in the Beatitudes. To wage that sort of love would be to end any conflict. Unfortunately the assumptions behind the slogan are that love is a matter of nice feelings and sensations—and presumably the judgment is being made that war has to do with nasty feelings and sensations. The truth with regard to war is otherwise. War is usually about matters of substance. There are realities, issues, and actions that give rise to the feelings. If we are to wage love in the world, that love must have substance and content also. It is interesting to note that the word "love" is not mentioned in the Beatitudes. On the other hand, as I have just suggested, the Beatitudes are a set of statements that spread out the content and substance of true Christian love. By all means let us make this sort of love!

Jesus did not say *"Blessed are the peace-lovers"* but *"Blessed are the peacemakers."* The difference is far reaching. We are probably all peace lovers. Of course we don't want any trouble, especially if it falls upon our own heads. We may disturb the peace of others, but none of us wants our own peace to be disturbed. We all want peaceful lives. But to set out to actually *make* peace is a very different matter. Nor is it likely to bring much peace to ourselves (in the sense of freedom from trouble). When the young Moses tried to reconcile two angry Hebrews neither of them thanked him for his trouble! (Cf. Exod. 2:13-14.)

This emphasis on the *making* of peace points up the difference between the Hebrew and Christian understanding and the notion of peace held by Eastern religions. To those influenced by Buddhism and Hinduism peace can often relate to no more than a state of mind. One can develop a peaceful inner state while surrounded by unrighteousness on every side. This is not to be despised; nevertheless the Christian could not feel at ease for long when confronted by unrighteousness. To the Jew and the Christian, peace is about activity rather than an inner state. Indeed it has been rightly suggested that the opposite side of the coin of meekness is that the Christian channels his aggressions into such activities as the making of peace whether it be in the making and running of missionary hospitals or political activity or environmental campaigning or evangelism.

Some Christians would look at this Beatitude and say that it referred basically to preaching the gospel of peace and reconciling men to God. I believe that this distorts the sense of the words and overlooks the Old Testament background, against which Jesus spoke. Of course the Christian wants, first and foremost, to help people to find peace with God. But his brief from God is more comprehensive, and Jesus, in the Sermon on the Mount, stressed the importance of reconciliation between man and man (Matt. 5:21ff.). Nevertheless all disruption stems from the fact of sin within the human race, whether it is between men and God, or whether it is between man and man or whether it is within nature. This is a fundamental teaching of the Bible. Therefore the Christian would be attempting to botch up peace rather than make it if he left out the basic call for reconciliation with God.

This does not mean, however, that we cannot attempt to bring *shalom* until the gospel has been received. I know Christians working in such areas as the probation service, community development, famine relief, and so on. I do not see it to be their calling to *concentrate* on leading men to faith in Jesus Christ. I hope that they are praying for opportunities to give specific explanations of the love of God in Jesus, but I believe that their forms of service are not means to an evangelistic end, but ends in themselves. Peace needs to be brought to our world at a number of levels, for peace has to do with righteousness and this covers a man's health, his home, his opportunities to find fulfillment and spiritual as well as material well-being. And to *make* peace rather than to *bring relief* means that we must care enough to go back to the fundamental reasons for the lack of peace in the first place, and to do something about them.

It is here that Christians have often expressed their concerns too superficially. We have often been happy to have our social concern epitomized by work in the soup kitchen when it should have been expressed in the legislative assembly. And if there is to be activity in the legislative assembly there must be men and women who see themselves as called by God for such work. Their motive must not be to make reputations but to make peace through the political expression of a hunger and thirst for righteousness. It is probably true that the church should not have party politics in the pulpit, but it ought to have party politicians in the pews.

The peacemaking which Jesus commended and which brings the new happiness is not meant to be limited to the relationships of men and God and man and man. It is meant to be exercised in the realm of nature. The Greek word for "peacemaker" is only used in one other place in the New Testament. The reference is somewhat tantalizing:

> For in him all the fulness of God was pleased to dwell, and through him to reconcile to himself *all things*, whether on earth or in heaven, *making peace* by the blood of his cross. (Col. 1:20; *my italics.*)

These words of Paul deliberately indicate that the

reconciliation Jesus achieved on the cross and which he offers to us is to be understood in terms of outgoing ripples which affect the whole fabric of existence. It affects not merely all men but all things. Paul was consistent in his thinking here for in his masterpiece, the epistle to the Romans, he spelt out the full scale of sin's disruption through nature in these words:

> All of creation waits with eager longing for God to reveal his sons. For creation was condemned to become worthless, not of its own will, but because God willed it to be so. Yet there was this hope: that creation itself would one day be set free from its slavery to decay, and share the glorious freedom of the children of God. For we know that up to the present time all of creation groans with pain like the pain of childbirth. (Rom. 8:19-22 TEV.)

This passage is remarkable because it reveals an admission on Paul's part of what is called the problem of *dysteleology*. In other words Paul is looking at nature and the whole created order and saying that it is all out of true. We do not see the harmony and pattern in nature that we ought to see if it is to point to a heavenly designer. But the reason for this *dysteleology* is not that there is no heavenly designer, but that his supreme creation, having been given dominion over the created order, has set up in unruly competition. A disorientated man leads to a disorientated nature.

While I cannot yet plumb the full implications of this biblical claim, I can see evidence of mankind's disorientating affect on his world in the present environmental debate. We are learning from the ecologist that man can so easily throw the whole delicately balanced "ecosphere" out of true. The exploitation of one natural resource can affect the structure of the terrain, the health of living species, and the general balance of nature. This we are learning. All *things* need to find peace. The Christian as peacemaker has a brief that goes far beyond people.

No wonder then that Paul pictured the whole created order as longing for the arrival of God's "sons," and yearning to find the peacemaking freedom that came from "the children of God." And is it only a coincidence that Jesus said that the peacemakers would be "called sons of God"?

But once again we are left asking whether we have little more here than the agenda for a coffee-cup discussion. What can we do about this *shalom* type of peace? The answer again must surely be that we make it where we are. There was little point in talking about Middle East peace in a New York taxi. It could do little to change the realities in Palestine. Yet perhaps in that taxi we made some peace between ourselves—he a Jew and I a Christian.

We are all meeting people and encountering some parts of the created order every day. Our calling as Christians is to make peace in those areas. The making of *shalom*-peace requires us to put something into the relationship that makes it more prosperous and harmonious. This in turn requires that we have first made peace with ourselves. Some of the fiercest criticism, most hurtful disgust, and most vicious hatred that has come to me, has come from myself. The first Beatitude rules all these matters out of court. If I can only come to terms with my inner poverty and realize that in spite of it I belong to the kingdom of heaven and am loved by my heavenly Father, then there is no more fuel for these inner conflicts. The liberation this brings and the reality of peace that attends that liberation should equip me to make peace wherever I may be.

God brought order out of chaos in the creation. God's peacemaking children are called to continue making order out of chaos wherever they find it, whether it be with people lost in sin, or whether it be in community development, or whether it be in digging a garden, or whether it be in an international conference of nations.

*Shalom!*

# CHAPTER 10
## *A NEW HAPPINESS*

Despite the fact that many modern translations use the word "happy" to introduce each of the Beatitudes we must ask whether they are about happiness in any sense.

In this book we have looked at the territory covered by Christ's unusual statements. We have thought about our own continuing spiritual poverty. We have seen Christ advocating mourning, calling us to renounce aggression, and commending deep yearnings for righteousness. We have considered the needs to be merciful, and actively to make peace. And all the time the setting in which the Beatitudes were given was of a group of men set apart from the crowds and the curious, without the comfort of anonymity; and rumbling in the background is the probability of persecution.

What has this to do with what we think happiness to be? The answer, perhaps, is nothing. What the Beatitudes talk about is either a totally different sort of happiness or it is not happiness at all. I argue that it is a new happiness and that what we usually think of as happiness is an illusion.

Think for a moment of a wedding and all the things

we say to the bride and groom. We want them, like the ending of the fairy story to be happy ever after. But we know it cannot possibly happen. Even if their health is sound, their babies born safely, their children talented and fortunate, and their home comfortable; sooner or later tragedy in the form of illness, death, or separation will take place. The chances are that there will be plenty of traumas and crises ahead for every bride and groom. We know it; the vows about "till death us do part" say it; and yet we all pretend otherwise. We prefer the fool's paradise.

What is happiness? We assume we know, and yet when we are asked we usually find it hard to come up with clear-cut descriptions. Perhaps we are nearer a satisfactory use of the word when we can look back on a holiday and say it was a happy time—which usually means it was different from normal in a pleasant sort of way. Again we might describe someone as happy—which means that the person so described smiled a great deal, or was high spirited, or appeared quietly contented more often than not. Christians are sometimes heard to talk about "a happy time of fellowship" which probably means that they experienced the elation of group excitement or the comfort of companionship at some meeting or group activity.

Rarely do we think of happiness as a constant quality of life—usually as something that is over and above the normal.

I want to suggest that if we examine how we speak

of happiness we find that a great deal of the time we are talking about *escapism*. The happy time is usually an occasion or period when we are not aware of traumas, problems, difficulties, opposition, and so on. We speak of getting away from it all.

Now escaping from the harshest realities is not necessarily wrong. Indeed, at times, it is positively essential. Jesus took his disciples apart from the demands of their mission on several occasions. He himself would go apart from his followers for solitude and prayer. He was accused of social drinking and eating with undesirable people which showed he enjoyed being entertained. We all need recreation and respite from the pressure and routine of life. God has designed us to need sleep—and that certainly is, among other things, a form of escapism.

Nevertheless a happiness which *relies* on escape is bound to prove unsatisfying in the end. To take a melodramatic example. You can get high on some drugs but you will always end up low again—perhaps even lower than when you started. I began this book by admitting that for years my happiness depended on factors that had no permanence—such as youth, affluence, and esteem—and that a time came when I saw the shallowness of the basis for my sense of wellbeing. The basis for happiness must be secure if we are not, sooner or later, to meet a terrible disillusionment.

I believe we need to see this ever more clearly as our civilization enters a crisis era when many of the things we have taken for granted such as abundant, cheap food, low priced energy fuels, and prospects of ever increasing living standards, can no longer be taken for granted. Many today are calling for a change to simpler life-styles, and this means far more than not changing our cars regularly or cutting down on our wardrobes. It involves turning away from the diverting toys and trinkets which pour into our lives and supply us with pleasant escapes from reality.

The real world is one where men are trying to live together while at the same time trying to assert themselves as individuals. It is one where there is competition and stress. It is a world where we grow old, are taken ill, and where we eventually die. It is a world where we run up bills and have to earn extra to pay them. It is a world where nationalism and ideologies open up international rivalries, tensions, and conflicts. It is a world that could blow itself apart with the contents of its hideous arsenals. It is a world with awesome inequality between men and men, and those who have long been the deprived ones are harboring the hatreds and resentments that stem from generation after generation of suffering.

There is no escape from this world. It cannot be switched off like the television documentary that becomes too disturbing.

If we are to have a rock-firm happiness it must be one that has faced up to the reality of death and of living in the world as it is. It must be something more than a happiness based on idealism, for this is not a world where many ideals are realized. It must allow us a clear conscience when surrounded by what is wrong and by what is needy. It must be something that can keep us hopeful when we disappoint ourselves, which is not infrequent. It must, above all, be something that can help us to see the eternal God at work in his world, and which will enable us to draw as closely as we can to the one who is the source of all love, consolation, courage, and power.

That sort of happiness is the one of which Jesus spoke. It is not elation in escape, it is fulfillment through *engagement*. To engage ourselves as we are and to engage our world as it is, will not bring us much elation. It might indeed call forth opposition and rejection. It will certainly bring grief into our lives. But this engagement is not only with ourselves and our world—it is also with our God. He is supremely the engager. When he came among us in space and time in the person of Jesus, he came as a suffering servant. We accept ourselves as we are because God does. We open ourselves toward a world that needs righteousness, mercy, and peace—because that is what our heavenly Father does. And as we identify with the ways of God we shall experience nothing less than the companionship of God. This experience of closeness is clear in the Beatitudes. When we read "theirs is the kingdom of heaven" we are reading about belonging to the King and being a part of his plans. When we read that the mourners "shall be comforted" we are reading a translation that hides something in the original Greek of the text. The word for "shall be comforted" is a word linked to that used to describe the Holy Spirit. It literally means "they shall find someone alongside," and the Holy Spirit is described in the New Testament as the someone alongside. So we could go on seeing from the second half of each Beatitude the idea of companionship and closeness to God: the pure in heart will "see God," and the peacemakers will be called "sons of God." Finally, the idea of fulfillment is powerfully portrayed in these words: "Blessed are those who hunger and thirst for righteousness, for they shall be satisfied." The Greek word for "satisfied" has the sense of being positively sated!

The Beatitudes therefore provide us with the sure basis for the sort of happiness that can ride the storms and give fulfillment and purpose. But if we want this new happiness, we have to embrace the call to a way of life which is radically different from other people. We have to accept what is little short of a reversal of the values and folk wisdom of those around us. There are no short cuts to the new happiness. It is the by-product of the new life of Christ's new people. Its motivation is not the desire for happiness but the desire to follow Jesus.

And this is what it is all about—following Jesus. Doctrine, theoretical belief, is a handmaid whose sole justification is to help us see who it is we are following. Prayer and pious practices are ways in which we draw more closely to Jesus, worship him, and "feed on him in our hearts by faith." But following him in the way we live is what Christianity, and the happiness it brings, is all about. The study of doctrine and the attendance at the prayer meetings or places of worship can become little more than religious forms of getting away from it all unless they are component parts of a life of following Jesus.

\*

In every age and for every generation the pattern of that Galilean hillside is repeated. Jesus sits apart from the crowds and yet in full view. He invites those who want to identify with him to come apart and hear what he has to say. It begins with the assurance that although all of us are poor in spirit we are welcomed, forgiven, and placed within God's plans. He goes on to hold out before us a totally new way of living.

Each one of us has to make up his own mind. We can choose to stay sheltered from his gaze and challenge along with the vast majority of our fellow men. Curious perhaps—catching snatches of what he is saying and maybe even agreeing, but preferring to be one of a crowd uncommitted and uninvolved.

Alternatively we can edge our way clear of those who want to remain in their uncommittedness and make our nervous way up the slope to listen, to identify, and to follow. This following will take us back down the slopes and fully into the world we may have thought we were leaving behind. But there will be one significant difference. We will experience the reality of Jesus' words: "Lo, I am with you always, to the close of the age" (Matt. 28:20).

That is the secret of the new happiness!

# STUDY GUIDE

## 1. OUT OF THE FOOL'S PARADISE

In his opening chapter, Gavin Reid shares his story of his own quest for happiness and his own definitions of happiness—and false happiness. Think back over your life: How have you defined happiness at various times? How have you known when you were or were not happy? What kinds of events have jolted you out of your happiness as Reid's awareness of possible war jolted him? Try writing down some answers to the above questions. Keep your notes for later use.

## 2. THE CHRISTIANS, THE CROWDS, AND THE CURIOUS

Reid suggests that Jesus Christ delivered the Beatitudes to "Christians, crowds, and the curious." In which of these groups do you belong? Why? In what ways does a careful examination of your life style permit you to pronounce this judgment upon yourself, as Reid suggests?

Think about the church of which you are a member. Ponder the type of "corporate new identity" it provides for you. Cite some specific ways that you and the members of your Christian community are held together by "commitment to the Master's life-style."

List twelve ways you would change your life-style if you were to become a "living epistle" of Jesus Christ. If you can think of no needed changes, what might this say about you?

## 3. THE TRUTH ABOUT OURSELVES

If someone asked you to answer the question, Who are you? how would you answer if you were not permitted to answer in terms of your family or occupation?

Reid writes that the problems of identity, mortality, and sin force us to hide from reality. What additional problems would you add to this list of those that make you a "tangled mixture of emotions, conflicting personalities, continuous selfishness and more?"

Try your hand at summarizing: Write a paragraph that summarizes what you now understand about the First Beatitude as a result of reading this chapter.

## 4. THE TRUTH ABOUT OUR WORLD

What do you do to avoid the reality of the world? Reid holds that all of us resort to escapism to avoid getting involved in a less-than-perfect world, but some of us seek to escape even the fact of our escapism. Take a hard look at yourself; be honest: What is this chapter and the words of the Beatitudes on which it is based saying to you?

Define in your own words *affectlessness*. Is ours an age of affectlessness? Cite some evidence and some reasons for answering as you do.

Write down some definite ways in which you can begin to "go headfirst into it all"—that is, begin to get directly involved in the needs and cares of the world, and by so doing find yourself "close to the heart of almighty God." Share what you've written with a friend, perhaps asking for that person's prayerful support.

## 5. ACHIEVEMENT WITHOUT AGRESSION

"We see power—the power to destroy obstacles in our path—as the way of getting things done." Reflect on your own life in terms of this statement. What kinds of power have you employed to achieve your ends? What kinds of power have been used against you? Describe examples from your own life of the "inevitable" power of meekness.

Answer in detail: What specific things can you do to "put on" the Christian qualities of love and gentleness?

Reid holds that "we are meant to pour out our anger toward God himself." Consider this idea carefully; put it into practice the next time you feel anger. Share the results of your experience with a friend.

## 6. RIGHT IS MIGHT

Write a one-paragraph definition of "righteousness," basing your definition on your understanding of the word prior to reading this chapter. Now, reread the entire chapter. Again, write a definition of righteousness, this time building your definition around new insights gained as a result of reading this chapter carefully. How are your two definitions alike? How are they different?

"It is not righteous that there should be great disparities in personal wealth." Do you agree with this statement? Why or why not? If you do agree, what can you do to bring more righteousness to your community?

If righteousness means living according to God's requirements, how can you be sure what God requires in each situation?

## 7. THE GODLY INFECTION

Draw a vertical line down the center of a sheet of paper. At the top of the page on one side of the line write the word "Rights." At the top on the other side of the line write

"Mercy." Next, write a brief definition of each term, directly under the term. Base your definition on your understanding of Reid's use of these terms. Then, write a description of a situation in which you acted or were treated on the basis of "rights" and a situation in which you acted or were treated "mercifully." Conclude your comparison of these two terms by describing your best understanding of God's relationship with us, his children.

Discuss this statement with several friends: "The ideal Christian fellowship will not be placid—but it would be merciful."

## 8. THE PURE AND THE PRUDISH

Christ insists on "inner purity" as a goal for the Christian. Is inner purity possible? How can you control thoughts and feelings in order to ensure inner purity?

How should a Christian who seeks the goal of purity relate to an "impure" society? By witnessing against it? By separating himself or herself from it? Or how? Write your answer, then list reasons for answering as you do.

Reid holds that inner purity may be strengthened by "crowding out" the impure, rather than "keeping out" the impure. Does this mean immersing yourself in a frantic schedule of church activities? Explain your answer in as much detail as possible, then discuss it with a friend.

## 9. MAKE PEACE, NOT LOVE!

Think for a moment of a situation in which you have found yourself "out of peace"—perhaps within your family, at your place of employment, or in a neighborhood conflict. What could you have *added* to that situation that would have waged peace effectively? Think as carefully and as critically as you can, then evaluate Reid's contention that peace is most successfully waged by *addition*. How would you explain this idea? Try doing so.

Talk with your pastor or with those in your church responsible for social action about the difference between "making peace" and "bringing relief." Which is your church doing primarily? What might your church do about the condition Reid calls "dysteleology"?

## 10. A NEW HAPPINESS

After reading the first chapter of this book, you thought about some of your understandings of happiness. Think again about this subject, writing our your definition and understanding of happiness as a result of reading this book. Carefully compare your earlier understandings of happiness with those you now hold. How are these understandings similar? How are they different? How can you translate intellectual differences into life-style differences?

Conclude your study of this book by preparing a set of goals for yourself that will lead you toward what Gavin Reid describes as the "new happiness"—closer companionship with God.